CRIMINAL JUSTICE

DANTES/DSST* Study Guide

© 2018 Breely Crush Publishing, LLC

DSST is a registered trademark of The Thomson Corporation and its affiliated companies, and does not endorse this book.

971083115143

Published by Breely Crush Publishing, LLC
10808 River Front Parkway
South Jordan, UT 84095
www.breelycrushpublishing.com

ISBN-10: 1-61433-044-1
ISBN-13: 978-1-61433-044-8

Printed and bound in the United States of America.

*DSST is a registered trademark of The Thomson Corporation and its affiliated companies, and does not endorse this book.

Table of Contents

🎓 *Criminal Behavior*

WHAT IS CRIME?

Simply stated, crime is the violation of criminal law. Those criminal laws can come from the Federal Government, or the State in which the crime occurred, or the local jurisdiction. Crime varies from shoplifting to murder, the ultimate violation of society's norms. An even better way to define crime is to look at the elements of a crime.

In the United States all crimes share certain elements. Obviously the first element of crime is the criminal act itself, also referred to as the ***actus reas*** (guilty act). In order to fulfill this element of crime an *act* must have been committed. Telling the police that you are a drug user doesn't *necessarily* mean that the actus reas is present. It could just mean you are a pathological liar. However, informing the police of a potential crime could open up an investigation to discovering a "guilty act" actually did take place.

The second element of crime is ***mens rea*** or guilty mind. This is looking at whether the criminal act was intentional and done with the knowledge of it being wrong. When you see people pleading insanity, they are claiming that they didn't have the mental capacity to "know better" or to possess a "guilty mind." Throughout the past several decades, this element of crime has evolved to encompass blameworthiness or whether the person who committed the act should be held responsible for it. This evolution of mens rea has allowed for negligence to be considered criminal.

Yet another element of a crime is **concurrence**. Concurrence is where the act and the intent of the crime intersect. This simply means that the actus reas and the mens rea must be present together, concurrently. Arguing the presence of concurrence is a difficult scene that plays out in many courtrooms. For instance, Mr. Criminal is on his way to work thinking about how much he hates Mr. Victim, possibly even plotting Mr. Victim's demise. During his commute, Mr. Criminal unintentionally runs a red light and t-bones another car only to discover Mr. Victim was in the other car and subsequently died. Because there was no concurrence; or no intention for the act to occur along with the act occurring, Mr. Criminal could argue that no crime was committed, or at least not the crime of murder.

Many criminal justice scholars believe the three elements just discussed are complete. Others, however, see crime as more complex and include additional elements of crime.

Harm is the first of these potential additions to the elements of a crime. A harm must have occurred for a crime to be present. The harm in victimless crimes (prostitution, gambling, etc.) is considered more of a social harm than a personal one.

Modern scholars also recognize **causation** as an element. Causation refers to the need for the *harm* to have directly been caused by the *actus reas* (guilty act). For example, Mr. Criminal intended to kill Mr. Victim in a knife assault but merely wounded him, sending Mr. Victim to the hospital and confining him to a wheelchair. Five years later, Mr. Victim dies due to complications (blood clots). The prosecutor would more than likely go back and charge Mr. Criminal with murder and the defense would have to argue that the blood clots that killed the victim were unrelated to the original assault.

Legality is also considered by some to be a necessary element of crime. Quite simply, this term means that an act must be against the law to be considered a crime. A law must have been "on the books" at the time of the act for it to be considered illegal.

The final possible element to be considered is **punishment**. This idea states that in order for an act to be considered a crime, a punishment must be in the law. For example, simply stating that theft is a crime is not enough, potential punishments must be in the law books for it to be so.

THEORIES OF CRIME

Much thought and study have gone into uncovering why people commit crime. The scientific study of crime and applicable criminal theories is known as **criminology**. Good criminological theory attempts to explain the causes of crime in scientifically tested hypotheses. This means that while everyone may have an idea of why people commit crimes, the most scientifically accurate theories bear the most weight. As time goes on and our world gets more and more advanced, the research behind criminological theories too becomes more advanced and scientific.

From the time a criminologist forms a hypothesis or an educated assumption about criminal behavior, until the idea evolves to a respected theory, much testing and evaluation must be done. First, in the process of developing a criminological theory, an observation is made. In the development of strain theory, for example the theorist may have realized that people below the poverty line are more prone to stealing than those with a higher disposable income. Second, this observation raises questions. Why, for example, are poor Americans caught stealing exponentially more often than their middle class counterparts? Next, a potential theory is developed. Poverty leads to a lack of opportunity, which leads to reduced success and corresponding wealth. The absence of success and wealth leads the poor to be frustrated and feel bad about their situation, eventually leading them to commit crimes to possibly elevate them to the same levels as their privileged counterparts. Simply developing this theory, however, is not enough. Criminal theorists must test their theories to be sure they are not flawed. They may research statistics, run experiments in different geographical areas and among different demographics; all to ensure their theory is logically and scientifically sound.

Finally, the theory can be presented in a manner acceptable within the criminological community.

Most current criminological theories can be traced to two original schools of thought: the **Classical** and **Positivist** theories. Both of these schools of thought came to the forefront in the late eighteenth and early nineteenth century.

Classical theory was led by Italian Cesare Beccaria. Beccaria explained criminal behavior in a simple hedonistic evaluation. He stated humans acted a certain way because they got pleasure from it. The idea of free will is central to this school of thought, that people commit crimes simply because they want to. Classical theorists also believe that we are all equal under the law and punishment should be meted out according to the crime. Because criminals were seeking pleasure, classical theorists rationalize that the punishment should inflict pain to outweigh any potential pleasure derived from the commission or spoils of the crime. This punishment will also serve as a deterrent to potential criminals.

Positivist theory was developed by another Italian criminologist, Cesare Lombroso. Lombroso believed that criminals committed crime because of their sociological surrounding and biological predispositions or physical characteristics. This school of thought looks more at the people behind the criminal act and determines that the criminals are, in a sense, victims of society, heredity, and their own environments. Positivists believe that the punishment should fit the criminal, rather than the crime, and that, due to our differences, punishments would differ from person to person.

Since these two schools of thought originated and criminology progressed and developed, many more theories were developed. You will see the origins of several of these theories are deeply rooted in the classical and positivist schools of criminological thought.

Biological theory, an old and since dismissed school of thought, was the belief that a criminal gene is present in people who commit crime. This line of thinking led to eugenics or the weeding out of undesirables. Studies were done and advocates of this theory believe they found that criminals actually had different bone structures and even different skull shapes than those of us law abiding citizens. Obviously, these theorists believed rehabilitation or treatment was fruitless and while criminals could be taught to re-direct their criminal behavior, they would never be cured of their criminality.

Sigmund Freud was an advocate of **Psychological** theory, sometimes referred to as psychoanalytical theory. He and others like him believed that all humans had criminal tendencies within them. However, throughout our childhoods we are conditioned to learn the difference between right and wrong. This theory states that adult criminal behavior is a direct result of poor relationships as children and a lack of parental guidance. Different to others, this school advocates intense therapy and potential rehabilitation.

Strain theory, also referred to as anomie or sociological theory, looks outside the criminal at his surroundings to explain his criminal behavior. This theory states that society and its organization or disorganization contributes largely to a person's criminal nature. This theory looks at socially acceptable goals and the means to achieve them. For instance, in the United States wealth is a socially acceptable and always pursued goal. Owning a home, investing money, driving a car, all are part of the "American dream." Strain theory looks at how this American dream is marketed as attainable for all and then looks at those Americans who have roadblocks preventing them from getting this dream. In essence, crime is committed when a citizen feels he has no other route of attaining socially acceptable goals.

Social Learning theory states we learn what is acceptable from the people around us. By human nature, we are involved in groups. Whether the group is a positive peer group (i.e. softball team), family, or negative peer group (i.e. gang), we learn what is acceptable behavior from our exposure to these groups. This is where criminals learn that criminal behavior is acceptable, at least under certain circumstances. According to this theory, those of us who surround ourselves with positive groups or are raised in a positive family group will not commit crime. However, people who surround themselves with deviant groups and people who think crime is acceptable will be much more likely to commit crimes themselves. This school of thought is one that is particularly popular when studying criminology and the juvenile offender.

Labeling theory looks at how society's labels affect a potential criminal. It states that the label "criminal," given to a person by society, encourages that person to become the label that has been imposed upon them. This theory looks at how society decides what will be a crime or considered deviant behavior and then labels it as such. Once this label has been attached to an act, it now becomes so. Meaning, a person who as a child displays rambunctious and rowdy or questionable behavior may be called deviant. People may expect this child to follow a certain criminal path into adulthood. Because society labeled this person, he or she will fulfill the label because other routes have been blocked. Once someone has been labeled deviant or criminal, we are less likely to give them opportunities that would contradict that assumptive label.

Control theory does something none of these other theories do. Instead of considering what causes people to commit crime it examines what keeps people from committing crime. Similar to Freud's psychological theory, control theories have a basis in the belief that all humans have criminal tendencies. Control theory looks at two types of controls, internal and external. Internal controls are those within us. Commonly referred to as self control, internal controls are those that we impose on ourselves. We might want a new car, know that stealing it is much easier than purchasing it, but our internal controls tell us that is not the right thing to do. External controls are those outside of us. Parents, law enforcement, school officials, employers, and family members can all play the role of external controls. They are the ones looking over our shoulders and paying attention to the choices we make. Control theory states that a lack of internal or external controls or a combination of both will open the door to criminal behavior.

Of course these are just several of the most popular theories. Emerging theories are always on the horizon. These few, however, have stood the test of time. Usually a combination of theories is used to discuss the cause of crime. There is no one right answer. These *integrated* theories are typically reliable in that they provide several cooperating reasons a person turns to criminality.

Good criminological theories not only help to explain why crime is committed. They also allow us to look deeper into how it can be prevented and what can be done to treat those people affected by it.

TYPES OF CRIME

There are several different ways to categorize crimes. We will look at the primary way that crimes are classified and then look several additional classifications. The first classifies crime according to its severity. This classification is useful in sentencing and organizing criminal law. The other categorization separates crimes by the criminal acts, who commits them, and who their victims are. In both instances, categorization of crimes has two purposes. First, we classify crimes to assist in organizing and compiling data. Second, we categorize crime to analyze causation and predict future trends.

The first way of categorizing is used every day in our court system and by the police in determining the severity of a crime. This is the most familiar way of classifying crime. The first type of crime under this model is the **misdemeanor**. A misdemeanor is a relatively minor offense. These minor offenses are punishable by a fine or *up to* one year incarceration. If sentenced to an active detainment, misdemeanants usually carry out this sentence in a local jail or work camp. Most often, however, misdemeanants receive suspended sentences or are given flexible options such as completing their jail sentence during weekends. Some basic misdemeanors include petty theft, simple assault, disturbing the peace, writing bad checks, and breaking and entering.

A **felony**, on the other hand, is the more severe classification of crime. A felony is an offense that is punishable by death or *more than* one year incarceration. These prison sentences are most often served at state or federally run facilities. Some areas of the country and even the Federal Court System have moved to classifying felonies according to severity. With potential sentences ranging from probation to death, these systems have found that further classification assists in determining the gravity of the crime. Felonies also typically carry with them a loss of certain rights. In most states, a convicted felon loses his right to vote, his right to bear arms, and the right to hold many professional licenses (i.e. doctor, dentist, attorney). Typical felonies include such things as assault, rape, murder, robbery, and arson.

Even more minor than misdemeanors are **infractions**. Infractions are extremely minor violations of law and are typically punishable by a small fine. You may have committed an infraction before and received a ticket with a date and time to appear and court. If you chose to waive this court date, you could simply send in payment for the fine. This is how most infractions are handled. Infractions include jaywalking, littering, and some traffic violations.

Sometimes in a class all by itself is **treason**. This offense, similar to espionage, involves a United States citizen who conspires with another country to in some way harm, wage war, or overthrow the United States Government. Treason has the same potential punishment as any felony with the greatest of these being death.

Now let's look at classifying crime according to the act itself, the victim, or the person committing the offense. There are many ways to classify crime in this regards. There is no single nationally accepted "list" of types of crimes. We will examine, however, a few of the well known types.

Organized crime is a popular term. It is popular and well known because there are so many movies about "gangsters" and so many popular songs that glorify the organized crime lifestyle. Organized crime refers to crime that is committed by an organized group of criminals, otherwise known as gangs. What was once attributed to the mafia, or other large, long standing criminal families has evolved into a problem reaching across age groups, nationalities, and all walks of life. Gangs support their ventures and are able to further recruit more members by generating an income. This income is typically tied to the drug trade, money laundering, illegal weapons, and racketeering.

White collar crime is, quite simply, fraud. The term "white collar" became popular because the offenders often committed or hid these offenses within the duties of their high level corporate careers. These crimes include embezzlement, credit card and check fraud, insurance fraud, bribes, tax evasion, kickbacks, and computer-related crime. Identity theft could also fall under the umbrella of white collar crime. According to the FBI, white collar crime costs the United States over $300 billion annually.

Victimless is a term used to describe crimes where there seems to be no victim. For example, prostitution is considered a victimless crime because both parties are consensual. Also, gambling is considered a victimless crime. One of the most controversial crimes in this category is illegal drug usage. Opponents of this term argue that there *is* a victim in this crime and that most often the victim is society. These opponents suggest that these "victimless" crimes slowly eat away at the moral fabric of our country. Some even believe that the "consensual" actors and the people they interact with are victims themselves.

When a family member commits a crime against another family member or significant other, they have committed what is called a **domestic** crime. Domestic cases are the largest group of violent crimes and they largely go unreported. This not only includes an assault between a man and a woman, but also includes assaults and neglect of children by a relative or caretaker.

Keep in mind that crime can be categorized in many different ways. One crime may nicely fall under several headings. Another crime may need a heading unto itself. Sex crimes, drug crimes, and street crimes are all other categories that could be expanded upon. The most widely approved and recognized way of categorizing crimes, however, is by their severity.

MEASUREMENT OF CRIME

Crime must be measured. Part of the benefits of categorizing crime is the ease by which it can now be organized and measured. Before we can organize and interpret crime, we need to compile the data. Compiling crime data has always presented difficulties. The nightly news is always filled with crime statistics, but in truth, these statistics are often flawed and don't paint a complete picture. The two largest sources of crime data use two completely different ways of compiling data. A newer, more concise source is also on the rise. All have their redeeming qualities and their shortfalls.

UCR

The FBI's **Uniform Crime Report (UCR)** was created in 1929 by an alliance of Police Chiefs who wanted a systematic and reliable way of compiling crime data. This alliance originally came up with seven crimes that it considered. In 1930 the first UCR was published. This initial publication included statistics submitted from 400 law enforcement agencies across the country. Annually, the FBI still gathers data from police agencies across the country in an effort to reliably quantify crime in the United States. The number of reporting agencies has increased to over 17,000.

In an effort to maintain consistency in reporting and the gathering of this data, law enforcement agencies receive training on the methods and terms used in the UCR. Although the states are not nationally mandated to report their data, most states have passed their own mandates.

In the original Uniform Crime Reporting Handbook, there were seven **index** crimes, also known as **Part I** offenses. These crimes would serve as the list of major offenses to be studied by the UCR. The original seven index crimes were: murder, rape, robbery, aggravated assault, larceny-theft, burglary, and motor vehicle theft. In 1979 an eighth crime was added to the index: arson. It is important to note that while the working definitions of the index crimes are similar to the statutory definitions, they are not considered the legal definitions for the crime. They serve only as working definitions in regards to the UCR.

The index crimes are further broken down by a classification. There are two classifications within the UCR and those are **property crimes** and **violent crimes**. Property crimes include burglary, larceny-theft, and motor vehicle theft. Violent Crimes include murder, forcible rape, robbery, and aggravated assault. Notice that the eighth index crime (arson) is not included in either of these classifications.

Local, county and state law enforcement agencies submit this data to the FBI in two ways. The first is as numbers of reported crime. These are cases that have come into the agency. For instance, if twelve rapes were reported in a small town, they would submit that figure to the FBI. The other figure submitted to the FBI is the **clearance rate**. The clearance rate refers to the number of those reported crimes that have been solved. By "solved" we mean they have resulted in an arrest (not necessarily a conviction).

The **crime rate** is a term often thrown around in the news media. The data collected in the Uniform Crime Report is used when calculating this rate. To find the crime rate in a specific geographical area you simply divide the number of reported crimes by the population of the sample area. You then take this quotient and multiply it by 100,000. This is the formula used when determining such things as Los Angeles' murder rate, or gang-related assaults.

For instance, the town of Thugsville had 12 murders last year. Thugsville's population is 26,000.

$12 \div 26,000 = 0.00046154\ldots$
$0.0004616 \times 100,000 = 46.16$

The murder rate in Thugsville is 46.16 per capita.

The UCR is also used in calculating the often cited **crime clock**. The crime clock is used when estimating how often a particular crime is committed. For instance, according to the FBI, in 2006 a murder occurred every 30.9 minutes in the United States. This is compared with one murder every 31.5 minutes in 2005 and every 32.6 minutes in 2004.

One problem with the UCR is uniformity. Although the FBI can suggest and urge departments to supply them with the data, some still do not. As stated before, participation is completely optional. Also, due to the variety of organizations reporting, the data submitted can be collected and interpreted in different ways depending on the department that is reporting it. The sheer number of agencies reporting can make absolute uniformity a near impossibility.

It is also assumed that occasionally crime statistics can be falsified by agencies for political reasons. By reporting a huge violent crime problem you can justify needing more funds to combat the problem.

Also, you may have noticed that drug offenses are not included in the UCR. This is a serious problem considering drug offenses account for the largest number of arrests and convictions in the United States. Also not included are Federal crimes.

The UCR does not account for the *dark figure of crime*. The dark figure of crime refers to those crimes that are never reported to police. Crime goes unreported for a variety of reasons. Domestic violence is one crime that officials believe goes largely unreported. Also, crimes committed by gang members or people of power in the community. Members of the community may fear retribution if they report a crime done in a crime-ridden neighborhood or a crime committed by a criminal organization.

NCVS

The **National Crime Victimization Survey (NCVS)** is a *self-reporting* survey developed in 1972 by the President's Commission on Law Enforcement and the Administration of Justice. This Commission, created under President Lyndon B. Johnson, was formed due to ever increasing crime rates. The Bureau of Justice Statistics (BJS) conducts the NCVS in an attempt to uncover the dark figure of crime. This survey method was not a new idea but this was the first large scale, government-sponsored self-reporting crime survey.

The NCVS is conducted by the BJS in cooperation with the US Census Bureau. A national sample of over 70,000 households is surveyed twice a year. Every three years this sample list is changed to provide the NCVS with fresh households and to continue a variety of sources. The Census Bureau selects the households randomly and every person over the age of 12 in the household becomes a part of the study. Each person is interviewed a total of six times over the next three years, twice in person and four times over the telephone.

The survey is not only comprised of yes and no questions related to victimization. The surveyors also gather data concerning the location of the crime, the suspect, whether the victim attempted to defend himself, if there was a relationship between the victim and suspect, and why the victim chose not to report the crime (if he in fact didn't). All of these questions, many of them recently added, attempt to clear up potential questions about the initial victimization statistics and seek to uncover any patterns in victimization and the dark figure of crime.

One of the unique problems with the data collected from the NCVS has been that the sources of information are the victims themselves. While this serves as the main focus of the survey (self reporting), it is also the number one problem. People have unique interpretations of events and often find it extremely difficult, if not impossible to view their own victimization in any sort of objective manner. Also, despite being given clear instructions, people will often give answers they think the surveyor wants to hear. There is also the tendency of some reporters to exaggerate or dilute the circumstances surrounding victimization.

No matter who is conducting the survey, some victims will still be reluctant to report incidences of victimization. This could be due to fear or the inability to interpret an act as a crime. For instance, a woman who is raped by her husband may not consider this a crime and although it would warrant reporting under the NCVS, she may refuse to do so out of protection for her relationship or due to her interpretation of what constitutes rape. Because of this, even with the NCVS, the dark figure of crime still exists.

NIBRS

The most recent crime data collection method is the **National Incident-Based Reporting System (NIBRS)** conducted by the Bureau of Justice Statistics. This system is fairly new and was approved for usage in 1988. It is very similar to the UCR and actually works directly with it. However, the NIBRS allows for much more detailed data than the UCR and is all done via computer.

The NIBRS categorizes crimes into two groups, group A and group B, with group B including the more serious crimes of the two. Also included in the NIBRS are drug crimes. This is a major improvement over the UCR.

While the NIBRS offers some improvement over the UCR, it still does not account for the dark figure of crime. Also, due to its relatively recent creation, many towns, cities, and states are still in the process of testing and adopting it for use. It is a voluntary program as well.

CRIME IN THE UNITED STATES

There are two ways an act becomes labeled a "crime" in the United States. The first is by becoming **statutory law**. Statutory law is the law "on the books." These laws are written by the Federal, State, or Local legislative bodies, empowered through the Constitution. Once a law is written, it is organized in a code. Federal statutory laws are organized in the United States Code (U.S.C.). State and local statutes are also organized into codes. Together, written and organized criminal law is known as the **penal code**.

The penal code includes two types of laws applicable to the criminal justice system and its application of the criminal law. These two types of laws in the penal code are *substantive* and *procedural* law. **Substantive** law defines exactly what a crime is and what the potential punishments for it are. **Procedural** law dictates how violations and court proceedings surrounding the violation are to be handled.

The second way an act becomes labeled a "crime" is by being established in **case law**. Case law is law that is dictated by judicial officials in their interpretation of statutory law. Case law is also known as **common law** and had its origins in the court systems of England.

The system of common law originated in the 13th century in England, when the king began sending out representatives to various independent courts to ensure that they were correctly enforcing the laws which he set forth. A common law system operates on the basis that throughout the land the same laws are used in governing, but that the judges may interpret the laws in consideration of the specific circumstances of the case. Common law systems contrast with civil law systems which extensively classify every type of crime and its associated punishment, not allowing room for interpretation.

Case law works under the law of **precedent**. Precedence ensures prior judicial interpretations and decisions are considered and adhered to in future similar cases. The law of precedence is derived from *stare decisis*, or to stand by what has been decided. Precedence ensures that Courts within the United States practice consistency. When someone cites case law they will cite the actual case it was taken from (i.e. Roe v. Wade).

JUVENILE DELINQUENCY

Juvenile Delinquency can be defined as action by a juvenile that violates juvenile status offenses or criminal law, or could be considered anti-social. This area of the Criminal Justice system is not only a concern for law enforcement and the Courts, but also weighs heavy on the mind of parents and society as a whole. Delinquency among children is nothing new. The methods of dealing with juvenile offenders, however, have changed dramatically over time.

HISTORY

The roots of our current system can be found in ancient Rome. The principle of *patria postestas* stated that the father of the household had absolute control over everyone else in the household. This control reached from the children to the wife and the slaves. Fathers, with this absolute power, had the right to sell, abandon, or even kill their own family. This ancient doctrine evolved into *parens patriae* in English Common Law.

Parens patriae translates to "father of the people" and refers not only to the head of the household, but the role of government. This principle allowed for the King (or his representatives) to step in as a paternal figure in the lives of juveniles who broke the law. This meant that the King was the father over the country and subsequently had parental rights over all of the citizens.

Another body of influence in the early juvenile justice system was the Church. In the Middle Ages, it was the Church that determined children under the age of seven were incapable of reason and therefore could not be held responsible for spiritual wrongdoings. Subsequently, acting upon the direction of the Church, English government held that children under seven could not be held responsible for crimes. Children from seven to the age of fourteen were afforded special treatment and were only treated as adults (in a criminal situation) under certain circumstances. At the age of fourteen children became adults in the eyes of the law.

Juvenile systems in the early United States were modeled after these systems in Great Britain. Like Britain, American juveniles were often subject to imprisonment and harsh punishments. Consistent with Puritan beliefs, the early punishments for juvenile delinquency were often severe in an effort to protect society from God's wrath, which could be brought down by spiritually irresponsible family units.

In the nineteenth century the United States was changing. The immigrant population was booming and new Americans were trying with all of their might to create a decent life for their families. Children were working alongside their parents in sweat shops and assembly lines. Families sacrificed education for their children in exchange for an additional income.

It was during this time that the first **house of refuge** was created. In an effort to save children from a life of crime and poverty, these houses were shelters filled with children. The living conditions of these homes quickly deteriorated with their overpopulation. What began as a way to keep children out of trouble became a breeding ground for young thugs.

Following the failed houses of refuge was the **Chicago Reform School**. This reform school and others like it to follow were designed to create the environment of a Christian family home for children who were seen as criminals in the making. The thought was that by providing children with structure and religion, delinquency would be prevented. Like the houses of refuge, the conditions in reform schools quickly deteriorated into homes that no longer reflected the original goal.

All of this eventually led to the creation of a juvenile court in Illinois dedicated solely to the needs of the juvenile delinquent. Following the lead of many states, in 1938 the

Juvenile Court Act was passed by the federal government. There were several principles that went into the creation of the Act.

- The belief that the government should act as a supreme parent to its children.
- The core belief that children should be saved and that, whenever possible, non-punitive actions should be used to "save" the child.
- The belief that children need nurturing.
- That each child's situation should be handled separately as children are all different and deserve individual attention.
- That because the court acted primarily to help (and not to punish), necessary non criminal procedures could often result in the constitutionally defendable denial of due process.

Due to the variety of reasons a child might enter the juvenile justice system, there are many categories used to describe the children under the care of the state.

1. **Delinquent** children are those who violated criminal law.
2. **Undisciplined** children are those who can't be controlled by their parents. This could be evident through behavior exhibited at school or in social situations.
3. **Dependent** children are those who have been abandoned or had no one to care for them.
4. **Neglected** children are those who do not receive proper care from their parents or guardians.
5. **Abused** children are those who have been physically, emotionally, or sexually abused at home.
6. **Status Offenders** are those who have committed offenses that are only considered crimes due to the offender's age. For example, truancy.

THEORIES

As with typical criminal behavior, much time has been dedicated to trying to explain why juveniles commit crime. Several theories have been proposed to explain why these children give into crime.

One of the first efforts at explaining youth crime was the **social ecology** approach, which attributed delinquency to social disorganization. **Social disorganization** exists when a group faces great change, inability to adapt, disharmony, and conflict. A contributing factor to social disorganization and thus juvenile delinquency is poverty. Poverty-ridden geographical areas are prone to conflict and population turnover, which according to social ecology theorists result in social disorganization.

You can see efforts at controlling social disorganization today. Inner city youth clubs and community centers that attempt to provide some stability to poor neighborhoods are seeking to provide community members with unity and a route to success. These organizations started when Clifford Shaw and Henry McKay, developers of the social ecology theory, created the first organization of its kind in the Chicago Area Project in the 1930s.

In the 1960s **opportunity theory** began making waves. Opportunity theory attributes juvenile delinquency, and other crime as well, to the lack of opportunities provided to lower class youth. This idea is that youth are encouraged to create goals and to strive for things that some of us middle class citizens take for granted (homes, cars, nice clothes, etc). But, unlike middle class children, these lower class kids aren't given access to the opportunities to make these goals a reality. This conflict leads juveniles to come by their opportunities via illegal means.

Opportunity theory gave rise to programs that attempted to equip poverty-ridden youth with the opportunities and chances to reach their goals legitimately. Job and skills training, and education assistance programs are all aimed at giving opportunities where they normally may not exist.

Age of onset is the age at which a child/teen first exhibits delinquent behavior of a criminal nature. The earlier the age of onset, the more frequent, varied and long lasting the criminal career. Poor parental discipline and monitoring are the biggest impacts in delinquent behavior.

WHAT CRIMES ARE THE YOUTH COMMITTING?

Juvenile crime runs the gamut, similar to adult crime. From simple theft to drug possession, assaults, burglary, and even murder, youth offenders are not immune to even the most heinous of crimes. Trends exist, however, that are unique to juveniles.

The Office of Juvenile Justice and Delinquency Prevention (OJJDP) acting with the UCR is the National source of data on juvenile crime. Similar to the UCR, the OJJDP collects information from law enforcement agencies on an annual basis. Also similar to the UCR, the reporting of juvenile offenses to the OJJDP does not include drug offenses, a common problem among youth offenders. However, the OJJDP only publishes a report on their findings once every four years.

Self-reporting surveys are a popular way of gathering statistics on youth drug usage. In the past several years, youth drug usage has shown a slow decline overall. However, juvenile drug usage is still at high levels and remains a concern for law enforcement, school officials, and parents. One reason drug usage among youths should be monitored so closely is the connection drug usage has with other crimes. Whether under the influence or in pursuit of drugs, youths (and adults) who have drug problems are more likely to engage in criminal activity.

Gang violence is another crime prevalent among youth. Oftentimes when looking for support and camaraderie, youth get involved in gangs that provide a false sense of family. Being in a gang leads to criminal activity and the means by which to commit it. If your support system is made up of criminals then it would make sense and would seem acceptable to become a criminal yourself.

While juveniles commit crimes similar to adults, there are a few differences. Interestingly, one of the biggest differences is the time of day that crimes are committed. With adults, the majority of criminal behavior takes place after dark. With youths, violent crimes peak between the hours of 3 pm and 4 pm, just after school lets out. Also, with youths, 1/3 of crimes committed occur between the hours of 3 pm and 7 pm.

In loco parentis is a legal term used to describe situations in which a person takes over the duties of a parent for a child (or otherwise incapable individual). *In loco parentis* is specifically used to describe more informal and temporary situations. For example, a babysitter acts in loco parentis when they are caring for children. The most common use of the term is to describe the relationship between teachers and students. It is the responsibility of the teacher to ensure the safety and health of the children when they are in their care. In both examples, the parent is essentially delegating responsibility temporarily.

In loco parentis should not be confused with the term parenspatriae. Parenspatriae is used to describe situations in which the government intervenes to ensure the health and safety of a child or individual when they are not being adequately cared for. The idea behind the parenspatriae doctrine is that the government is the ultimate "parent" or protector of all individuals and it is their right and duty to step in when parents are irresponsible.

IMPORTANT COURT CASES AFFECTING JUVENILE OFFENDERS

Kent v. U.S. (1966)

Morris Kent had committed several burglaries and purse snatchings when he was just fourteen. At the age of sixteen, however, Kent entered a woman's apartment, stole her wallet, and raped her. His fingerprints were found at the scene and he later confessed to the crime.

Prior to trial, Kent was subjected to several psychological and psychiatric evaluations and found to be suffering from severe psychopathology. The judge on the case, however, refused to listen to the mental health professionals and Kent's attorneys and determined that Kent would be tried as an adult. The judge failed to give reason for this decision. Kent was found guilty and sentenced to prison for 5-15 years on eight counts. Kent's lawyers appealed his case all the way to the U.S. Supreme Court, who sided with Kent in that he was denied an adequate hearing at the juvenile court level and the transfer of his case to adult court was unfair.

This case was important because it brought to light the need for due process in juvenile court hearings for the first time. It cemented a proper procedure to be followed when moving a child's case out of juvenile court jurisdiction.

In Re Gault (1967)

Gerald Gault and his friend Ronald Lewis were put under arrest in 1964 for making prank phone calls to a neighbor woman. Gault was already on probation at this time for being with a different friend when that boy decided to steal a wallet.

Gault's parents were at work at the time of arrest and were not notified of the situation. Once they arrived home they had to determine where their son was and only did so with assistance from Ronald Lewis' mother. When they approached the police, Gault's parents were given no information. They were not told what the charges were or who the alleged victim was. They were, however, told when the initial hearing would be held.

At that initial hearing, only Gault and the juvenile officer gave testimony. Neither the complainant nor an attorney for Gault was present. The judge set a second hearing date. Mrs. Gault requested the alleged victim be present at that hearing so she could make a determination as to whose voice she heard on the phone that day. The judge denied Mrs. Gault's request. At that second hearing Gerald Gault was found guilty and sentenced to a boy's school until his 21st birthday.

Gault's attorney appealed his case all the way to the Supreme Court where he argued that Gault's constitutional rights had been violated and he was denied due process. The Supreme Court sided with Gault's attorneys on four key issues.

1. *Right to Counsel.* Gault was not informed of or given the opportunity to exercise his right to an attorney.
2. *Protection Against Self-Incrimination.* Gault was never informed of his right to remain silent or that his statements could be used against him.
3. *Right to Confront and Cross-Examine Witnesses.* The court failed to require the complainant's presence at the hearing.
4. *Notice of Charges.* Gault and his parents were not given enough notice to prepare for the hearing.

Now, juveniles are guaranteed many of the same rights afforded to adults and *In Re Gault* was partly responsible for setting this procedure-changing precedence. Other juvenile cases followed, further fine tuning the procedures for dealing with juvenile offenders, but this one laid the groundwork.

Criminal Justice System

HISTORICAL ORIGINS AND LEGAL FOUNDATIONS

Laws regulate relationships and have been around for centuries. The present day United States Criminal Justice system can most recently be traced to England and then further back to Rome, Egypt, and eventually Babylon. You see influences of these ancient systems alive today when speaking of broad concepts like law enforcement and court systems, and when discussing specific ideas such as the due process of law and "victimless crimes."

ANCIENT HISTORICAL FOUNDATIONS

Modern day criminal justice systems can be traced back to the ancient city of Babylon in 2000 B.C. At this time, the city was ruled by King Hammurabi. King Hammurabi was responsible for the earliest surviving body of law. The **Code of Hammurabi** was engraved on stone tablets. It was a body of 300 laws that established property and other rights. It included provisions for witchcraft, family laws, business and military regulations, wages, loans, debts, and taxes. This code was responsible for establishing the legal principle of *lex talions*, an eye for an eye.

The first court systems arose in ancient Egypt around 1500 B.C. The Pharaoh appointed judges to preside over the courts. Also in Egypt, around 1000 B.C. public officers performed police duties in an effort to enforce the laws of the land.

The most significant contributions to Western Law came from early Roman law. The origins of Roman law were the **Twelve Tablets**, a group of rules governing, religious, economic, and family life, created around 450 B.C. by a panel of ten of the wisest men in Rome. They were based on basic rules accepted for many years by tribes existing prior to the Roman Republic.

Later in Roman history, the influential Emperor Justinian I directed Roman laws be put into a set of writings. These laws, known as the **Justinian Code**, dealt with everything from the organization of the Roman State to the affairs of families. Unlike attempts at written law before, the Justinian Code recognized and separated the law into public and private law. Public laws dealt with the organization of the Roman government, while private law dealt with family affairs, contracts, possessions, and harms against people. The Justinian Code contained elements of what we know today as our civil and criminal laws and certainly influenced the development of the legal systems we see at work today.

In the mid-first century, Roman legions conquered Great Britain and ruled over the land. Roman authority, customs, and laws were forced on the English. As Great Britain evolved, so did their laws. Although American settlers were looking for a way out of England and to escape the King's rule, his law followed them and affected the law of America while it was under the throne and after we gained our independence.

FEUDAL LAW

Feudalism was the system of organization in Europe during the 9th to 15th centuries. It was a hierarchal system based on the relationship of the lord to the vassal (a servant or feudal tenant). Typically a lord possessed a good portion of land that was lived on by multiple vassals. In exchange for protecting the vassals and allowing them to live on his land, the vassals owed military service to the lord. The lowliest people on the land were the peasants. Finally, the lord was considered a vassal to his King.

Disputes between vassals were taken up with the lord and disputes between peasants were often taken up with the vassals. This sort of mediation seemed to work well for people of the Middle Ages. Although Feudal Law was never acknowledged in the United States, you can see its influence in sharecropping and slavery practices of earlier times.

COMMON LAW

English customs, rules, and judicial rulings all made up **common law**. It is an unwritten body of law. Common law originated when property disputes arose in England. The two disputing parties would go before a judge who would hear the evidence and make a ruling. This ruling would have precedence and became a piece of the common law. As the law further developed and disputes became more detailed and specific, the judges would fine tune decisions and make appropriate rulings based on the previous decisions along with their specific differences. Common law is the basis of modern case, statutory, and even criminal law. You can see its influence when a judge in Florida, for example, takes into consideration the ruling of a judge in Oregon on a similar case. In the United States, what was common law is referred to as **case law**. It was the law of the land, the unwritten and universally accepted rules.

MAGNA CARTA

The Magna Carta, created in 1215 under King John of England, was a written charter that bound the King by law. It arose due to disagreements between the King, the English Barons, and Pope Innocent III. It set forth specific royal concessions in an attempt to appease the Barons. A phrase that became popular with the Magna Carta was "the law of the land," which is included in the document itself. However, later in history it was used to support revolts against the King's rule; the interpretation changed with the times. It was then interpreted to give certain rights to individuals and more tightly bind the government. During the civil war era it was used to demonstrate how tightly bound by law the King was. In particular, a specific clause that was originally written to stop the King from persecuting the barons without good cause, was later interpreted into the original concept of "due process of law," guaranteeing some rules of fairness and regulation in respect to individual rights in the legal system. The document contained facets that became an important part of US law. First, it was a sort of declaration of rights. It restricted the powers of the king and required him to follow all laws as well as any other citizen. Second, the Magna Cart is the first document to refer to a due process of law which must be followed in the course of law enforcement.

NATURAL LAW

A discussion of the origins of Western Criminal law would not be complete without addressing the influence of religion. The majority of our historical documents and legal practices has its roots in the Christian principles that the nation was founded upon. For this reason, much of our criminal law is based on moral behaviors and what is "good" and "evil." Natural law can refer to many religious influences, but particularly refers to the moral law that is universally accepted. In Christian religions, this law can be seen in the Ten Commandments.

Natural law assumes that it is obvious some actions are wrong unto themselves, meaning they don't need a law for us to know they are wrong, that we as humans can recognize them as innately wrong. These acts are called ***mala in se***. You know these inherently wrong acts as murder, rape, arson, and other violent personal acts. Also included in *mala in se* are those acts that are "contrary to nature." Many states still have laws on the books that refer to the acts as "crimes against nature." Several of these crimes have been abandoned due to the evolution of sexual tolerance when speaking of homosexuality, and lesbianism, which were previously not tolerated and often persecuted as criminal acts.

Acts that are not natural law violations and are only wrong because the law says they are wrong are called ***mala prohibita***. *Mala prohibita* refers to laws that are on the books but may not be considered immoral if it weren't for the statute calling it so. Examples of laws that fall under *mala prohibita* are prostitution, drug usage, traffic offenses, and gambling. Notice many of these are what we refer to now as "victimless" crimes.
In English history the distinction between *mala in se* and *mala prohibita* was very important in determining punishments. The two classes were tried in different courts, with the less serious *mala prohibita* being tried by a justice of the peace imposing far less severe penalties.

ADMINISTRATIVE LAW

Administrative law is the branch of public law that deals with the powers and duties of government agencies that make public policies and rules that affect public health, safety, and environmental protection, Agencies such OSHA, and the EPA fall under administrative law.

U.S. CONSTITUTION

The U.S. Constitution is the groundwork that our Criminal Justice System is founded upon. Signed in 1787, the Constitution has the final say in questions of individual rights and the powers of the government. The highest Court of the land's sole purpose is to interpret and apply the rules of the U.S. Constitution to cases before it. The modern Criminal Justice system began with the Constitution and it is where we derive our legally granted rights and principles. Although the Constitution doesn't define any pro-hibited activities or tell us what is considered a crime, it is the standard that all criminal laws are held to.

Due Process

The idea of "due process" appeared in early America when the Magna Carta was con-sidered the law of the land. Early lawmakers considered it of the utmost importance that the people be protected from the powers of the government. The due process term, however, wasn't used until the ratification of the Bill of Rights in 1791.

The first eight amendments, included in the Bill of Rights, are probably the most cited in our Criminal Justice system. In particular the 4th, 5th, and 14th Amendments, which guarantee our right to **due process**, are the cornerstone of much of the system.

The most recognizable due process clause is in the 5th amendment, which states:

> …nor shall any person be subject for the same offence to be twice put in jeopardy of life or limb; nor shall be compelled in any criminal case to be a witness against himself, nor be deprived of life, liberty, or property, without due process of law…

A similar statement exists in the 14th Amendment:

> No State shall make or enforce any law which shall abridge the privileges or im-munities of citizens of the United States; nor shall any State deprive any person of life, liberty, or property without due process of law; nor deny to any person within its jurisdiction, the equal protection of the law.

Simply stated due process refers to the course of legal actions that follow the rules created for the protections of individual rights. To have a "right" to due process then means that we have a right, when being accused of a crime, to certain protections under the law. This is vitally important in the organization of a justice system and particularly when discussing human rights.

Within the 4th, 5th, and 14th Amendments are several rights granted to individuals that make up what modern-day Courts consider due process. Those include:

- Right Against Unreasonable Searches and Seizures
- Right to be Assumed Innocent until Proven Guilty
- Right Against Arrest Without Probable Cause
- Right Against Self Incrimination
- Right to Fair Interrogation by the Police
- Right to an Attorney
- Right to an Impartial Jury
- Right to be Present at Trial
- Right to Confront Witnesses
- Right Against Cruel and Unusual Punishment

This list is in no way exhaustive, but gives a good indication of what due process entails. Modern-day courts and criminal justice agencies are required to adhere to the due process rights.

Although one of the purposes of the Bill of Rights is to state the rights that allow people to act, another, possibly more important, purpose of the Bill of Rights is to ensure the rights of accused individuals, or restrict the actions of law enforcement. Several amendments deal with this issue, and not all of them are restricted to just the Bill of Rights Amendments. Some of the most commonly referenced amendments in the field of criminal justice are the Fourth, Fifth, Sixth, Eighth and Fourteenth Amendments.

The Fourth Amendment protects against unreasonable searches and seizures. Because of this amendment it is required that police officers obtain a search warrant before searching a suspect's property or taking any evidence. This protects the privacy of individuals, and is meant to ensure that innocently accused individuals are not treated unfairly. To obtain a warrant, the officer must be able to show that they have enough justification for suspecting the individual, and describe what it is that they expect to find.

The Fifth Amendment deals with legal procedures in criminal cases. The amendment requires indictment by grand juries, which determine whether there is sufficient evidence to accuse an individual; protects against double jeopardy, meaning that an individual cannot be tried twice for the same crime; protects against self-incrimination, which means the accused individual does not have to speak to law enforcement or testify against themselves; ensures due process, meaning that there are specific steps law enforcement must take in criminal cases; and addresses the issue of imminent domain, which requires that individuals be compensated when their property is taken for public use.

The Sixth Amendment lists a number of rights which are extended to accused individuals, including: a speedy trial, a public trial, a trial by an impartial jury of peers, to be told what there are accused of, to know of the witnesses against them, the chance to find witnesses in their defense, and the right to a lawyer.

The Eighth Amendment serves two purposes: to protect against cruel and unusual punishments, and to protect against excessive bail. The amendment does not go into great detail, but leaves the terms "cruel," "unusual," and "excessive" up to interpretation. Generally, the terms are considered to refer to situations that are degrading to human dignity, or of a severity that does not fit with the crime.

The Fourteenth Amendment has three important clauses: the citizenship clause, the due process clause and the equal protection clause. The Fourteenth Amendment was passed during the post Civil War Reconstruction Era of United States history. As such, the purpose of the citizenship clause was to extend citizenship to all former slaves, and the equal protection clause required that equal and fair treatment be extended to all citizens. Both of these clauses, therefore, had the purpose of extending equality to minorities. On the other hand, the purpose of the due process clause was to strengthen to requirement of due process mentioned under the Fifth Amendment by requiring of state governments in addition to federal governments.

The Miranda Rights consist of a list of rights that an individual must be informed of if they are taken into custody. Included in the Miranda Rights are those such as the right to remain silent and the right to an attorney. The purpose of the Miranda Rights is to ensure that individuals are aware of their Fifth Amendment rights, which protect against self-incrimination. Before it was required that individuals be read their Miranda Rights, many officers would take advantage of the fact that not all individuals knew what they were. A suspect must be informed of their Miranda Rights after they are taken into custody and before they are interrogated. This means that a person who has not been arrested can be questioned without being read their Miranda Rights.

The Miranda Right requirement, and its name, originated from the case of Miranda v. Arizona. In the case, the defendant, Miranda, was released due to the fact that he was unaware of his rights and therefore did not have an adequate chance to defend himself.

DUE PROCESS AND THE WARREN COURT

In the 1960s the United States Supreme Court solidified the importance of due process through a series of Court rulings. This era, known as the "**Warren Court**," was led by Chief Justice Earl Warren who was very concerned with protecting the people against the power of the government in criminal proceedings. At the time, several of these decisions were considered controversial, but Chief Justice Warren is known as one of the most influential figures in the modern day justice system.

Of significance were several cases including but not limited to:

- Brown v. Board of Education (segregation, civil rights)
- Gideon v. Wainwright (right to counsel)
- Mapp v. Ohio (search and seizure)
- Miranda v. Arizona (rights of the accused)
- Abbington v. Schemmp (separation of church and state)
- Katz v. United States (search and seizure, wiretaps)

The case of **Atkins v. Virginia** resulted in the Supreme Court ruling that it is against the Eighth Amendment for mentally retarded individuals to be given the death penalty. In the case, Daryl Atkins and a friend were tried for the kidnap and murder of an airman from a nearby Air Force Base. The evidence against them was overwhelming; however, Atkins was the one who had actually fired shots and the defense used previous IQ tests and school records to show that he was mildly mentally retarded and argued against the death penalty. The case went eventually to the Supreme Court which affirmed that the death penalty was not appropriate for mentally retarded individuals.

In the case of **Furman v. Georgia**, William Henry Furman broke into a house in the middle of the night to burglarize it. When the owner was awakened, Furman attempted to flee - accidentally discharging his gun and killing the owner. Because the death happened while a burglary was being committed, the law in Georgia constituted that this was a capital case, the death murder and was punishable by the death penalty. This was taken to the Supreme Court, arguing that the death penalty violated the Fourteenth Amendment. The Supreme Court overturned Furman's execution. It stated that unless a uniform policy of determining who is eligible for capital punishment exists, the death penalty will be regarded as cruel and unusual punishment.

In the case of **Mapp v. Ohio**, police had been tipped off that they could find evidence and a suspect in a bombing case at the home of Dollree Mapp. They entered the house, without a legitimate warrant. Mapp protested and the officers arrested her for belligerence. After searching they house they did not find the evidence they were searching for. Instead, they found pornographic material in a briefcase, which she insisted must have been placed there when she loaned it out recently. She was charged with possession of pornographic material and she was found guilty due to the evidence. She fought the charge on a basis of the Fourth Amendment protection against unreasonable searches and seizures, and argued that the evidence should be inadmissible. The Supreme Court decided in her favor ruling that evidence obtained in violation of the Fourth Amendment is inadmissible in court.

In the case of **Hudson v. Palmer**, Ted Hudson, an officer, searched the locker of Russell Palmer, an inmate in a Virginia prison. Palmer sued, arguing that the search was a violation of his Fourth Amendment rights. The result was a Supreme Court ruling that the Fourth Amendment does not apply to prison inmates. This means that if a prisoner feels that they are unfairly treated during a search of their cell, they cannot sue in federal court. Rather, they must sue in state court if they wish to recover damages.

The case of **Powell v. Alabama** deals with the rights established in the Sixth and Fourteenth Amendments. A nine black teenage boys were accused (under doubtful circumstances) by two girls of sexually assaulting them. The boys were taken into custody but a crowd formed and the Alabama National Guard had to be called in to protect them. None of the boys were allowed to contact relatives and were not given a chance to consult with lawyers or call witnesses. All the boys were convicted and eight received the death penalty. The convictions were appealed up to the Supreme Court which determined that states were required through the Fourteenth Amendment to ensure the rights to due process mentioned in the Fifth and Sixth Amendments. The most important issue considered was the right to legal counsel. The Supreme Court ruled that "a defendant, charged with a serious crime, must not be stripped of his right to have sufficient time to advise with counsel and prepare his defense."

In the case of **Gideon v. Wainwright**, Gideon was charged with a felony but was unable to pay to hire an attorney to defend him. The court refused to appoint him one because it was not a capital case. Gideon was forced to represent himself and was convicted and sentenced to five years in jail. On appeal, the Supreme Court ruled that under the due process clause of the Fourteenth Amendment, if a defendant was too poor to hire an attorney, the court must appoint one in any criminal case.

The case of **Terry v. Ohio** originated when a police officer stopped and searched three individuals, Terry and two friends, under suspicion that they were about to rob a store. He found a gun and had them arrested. Terry argued that the random searched constituted an unreasonable search and seizure and therefore it was a violation of the Fourth Amendment and the evidence found during it should not be allowed in court. The Supreme Court ruled that random police searches are perfectly legal, so long as the police officer has specific and articulable facts to support doing so.

The Eighth Amendment was called into question in the case of **Gregg v. Georgia**. In the case, Gregg was convicted of armed robbery and sentenced to death. He appealed, arguing that the death sentence constituted cruel and unusual punishment and was therefore illegal under the Eighth Amendment. The Supreme Court reviewed the case and held that the death penalty was not cruel and unusual punishment, but that it was also not appropriate in the specific case.

An important case in the treatment of juvenile crimes is that of **Kent v. United States**. Kent was arrested in connection with a possible robbery and rape of a woman at the time that he was 16. Because he was under 18, he was under the jurisdiction of the juvenile court unless they were to sign a jurisdictional waiver after investigating it themselves, which they did. However, Kent appealed on the basis that the waiver was invalid. The Supreme Court held the validity of the waiver and affirmed a number of procedures relating to it. For example, the ruling held that a full investigation must be held before a jurisdictional waiver is signed, there must always be a hearing when a jurisdictional waiver is considered, and that legal counsel must have access to their social records.

The application of due process is separated into two classifications that line up with two types of law. **Substantive due process** refers to the creation and definition of what a person's rights are, while **procedural due process** refers to the enforcement of the laws and the punishments for violations. What is included in the constitution's definitions of due process are mostly procedural. They dictate procedures that the government can and cannot go through when dealing with people and trying to remove a person's rights (for example: arrest and a person's right to remain silent).

Substantive due process is a little stickier and involves those rights that all people are entitled to that may or may not be written out but are accepted universally. It also states that sometimes the government cannot take away someone's rights no matter *how* they do it, but that they must have substantial *reason* to do it. For instance, the right to privacy is not explicitly stated in the US Constitution, but it is widely accepted as a human right and has been ruled as such through years of case law. The application of substantive due process when dealing with the right to privacy would cause the justice system to operate from what is known to be right due to precedence and case law, which was largely based on the universally accepted notion that people are entitled to privacy, although it is not a right written in the Constitution.

DUE PROCESS MODEL OF JUSTICE

There are two primary goals in crime control, one of which relies heavily on due process. The **due process model** of crime control emphasizes protecting individual rights at all stages in the Criminal Justice process. This means that from arrest to detention, all actors in the justice system are required to protect the individual's rights. A police officer is required to recognize those rights and protect them during arrest and questioning. The Courts, including prosecutors, are required to do the same during hearings and presentations of evidence. Corrections professionals are required to maintain those rights even during imprisonment, probation, and community supervision.

The other model of control is known as the **crime control model**. This model places its influence on efficient arrest and conviction of offenders. Advocates of the crime control model often think of due process advocates as easy on crime and too coddling to offenders. Critics of the crime control model say that it is at the other extreme, sacrificing crime control for human rights. While it has been contested that these two models are at such extremes that they cannot work in conjunction, more recent system analysts see that it is necessary to have a balance of the two models, controlling crime in an efficient manner while not losing sight of the rights that are guaranteed to all people of this nation.

ADMINISTRATIVE AGENCIES

The United States Criminal Justice System is organized into three sections:

1. Law Enforcement: Local, State, and Federal police
2. Courts: Local, State, and Federal Court systems, Courts of Appeals and the U.S. Supreme Court.
3. Corrections: Jails, Prisons, Community Supervision (probation), and other court sanctions

It is the goal of law enforcement to enforce the laws, the goal of courts to interpret the laws, and the goal of corrections to carry out a sentence provided by the courts.

U.S. Court System

Two distinct Court systems exist in the United States. The federal courts and the state courts have different purposes and for the most part act independently of one another. This unique dual court system was created from a desire to keep powers of the larger federal government under control.

FEDERAL COURT HISTORY

The federal court system was created by the Constitution. Article III, Section 1 dictates the creation of one Supreme Court and additional smaller courts as Congress saw fit. The Constitution also set forth the **jurisdiction** of the federal courts. Jurisdiction refers to the locations, types, and subject matter of court cases over which a specific court has the power to preside. Federal court jurisdiction, in the Constitution, includes federal laws, disagreements between states, and cases where one of the parties *is* a state.

FEDERAL COURT ORGANIZATION

Because of the powers granted to Congress within the Constitution, allowing them to create inferior Courts under the US Supreme Court, Congress has created a Federal Court system that includes three tiers:

1. U.S. District Courts
2. U.S. Courts of Appeals
3. U.S. Supreme Court

FEDERAL DISTRICT COURTS

There are a total of 94 district courts. These are not only in the 50 states but there are also federal district courts in the District of Columbia, Guam, Puerto Rico, the Virgin Islands and the Northern Mariana Islands. Many states have more than one district, but all have at least one. These courts have **original jurisdiction** over federal law violations. Original jurisdiction refers to the authority given to a court to be the first court to hear the matter.

District court judges are appointed by the President and confirmed by the Senate Judiciary Committee. They are often recommended to the president by senators or by members of the president's political party serving in the House of Representatives. Their term is lifelong, which means they can serve as long as they want, barring removal. Multiple district court judges serve in each district. Judgeships (new judicial openings) are created by Congress as needed.

U.S. magistrate judges are appointed by the District court judges and rule over cases as specified in statute and by the district court judges. These magistrates only serve a term of eight years. The magistrate's duties vary greatly from court to court. Some potential magistrate duties are holding arraignments, setting bail, or issuing warrants.

One of the judges, typically the one who has served on the court the longest, is designated the **chief judge** and performs administrative duties as well as hearing cases. A judge holds the chief judgeship for a term of seven years.

FEDERAL COURTS OF APPEALS

A group of federal judicial districts make up a **circuit**. Each circuit (there are thirteen) has a court of appeals. These courts are often referred to as "circuit courts." Historically, judges hearing appeals would travel to each district within the geographical region in a specific order, creating a circuit, hence the name.

Each court of appeals consists of six or more judges. The number of judges depends on the caseload of the Court. These judges are also appointed by the president upon recommendation by the Senate and are appointed for a life term. Similar to the district courts, one judge is designated as the chief judge.

An **appeal** refers to the request made to a higher court to review the findings of judgment from a lower court. These federal appellate courts have **mandatory jurisdiction** over cases heard in federal district court. This means that the federal appeals courts *must* hear the cases brought to them. Criminal appeals are typically heard by a panel of three appeals court judges, rather than a panel of all six.

The *Federal Rules of Appellate Procedure* dictate procedural rules for the federal appellate courts to follow. This body of rules is not exhaustive and each court may operate under additional "Local Rules." Local rules may refer to slight differences between circuit courts. For instance, perhaps one circuit values oral arguments while the other allows for a written disposition in their place.

Cases heard in the appellate courts include those that are frivolous and can be disposed of quickly as well as those that are significantly complex and require extensive questioning of law and policy. The latter type of case is typically riddled with disagreements between the courts, judges, and parties in the case. The possibility of a reversal of a district court's decision is most likely in these more complex cases.

THE SUPREME COURT

The United States Supreme Court is the highest court in the Nation. The court consists of nine Supreme Court Justices, each appointed by the President and appointed for life terms. Justices typically serve for a very long time, often well past what is typically considered retirement age. The average age of a Supreme Court justice is in the late sixties. The ninth Supreme Court justice is referred to as the Chief Justice and is nominated to that position by the President. The Chief Justice's term is life-long as well.

The Court's greatest power is in the power of **judicial review**. Judicial review means that the Supreme Court can evaluate and review any decisions and actions by any Court or governmental agency in the Country. This means that the Supreme Court, in a review of Constitutionality, can delve into decisions not only made by other Federal Courts, but also by State Courts, and even the executive and legislative branches of the government.

Although judicial review is not explicitly granted in the Constitution, it was considered and anticipated by the writers of the Constitution. This was anticipated because the original framers of the Constitution wanted to be sure that there were checks and balances in place for a legislature. Further ensuring judicial review's place in the Supreme Court was the case of *Marbury v. Madison* (1803), in which Supreme Court Chief Justice John Marshall cemented the authority of the Supreme Court as final interpreter of the Constitution.

An important case early in United States history was that of Marbury v. Madison. When Thomas Jefferson was elected to be the third President of the United States, the second President (and his political rival) John Adams made a number of last minute appointments, one of which was to Marbury. However, the paperwork was never delivered to him and Jefferson later appointed Madison to the same position. Marbury sued, and under the laws of the day did have legal precedence for doing so. The Supreme Court ruled that he did have a right to the position. However, they also ruled that the Constitution did not give the court the right to force the point, and stated that it was their right to determine whether or not certain acts of Congress or the President were Constitutional. This power of reviewing acts of the other branches has come to be known as the power of judicial review and is an important element of the judicial branch today.

The Supreme Court hears cases that are high level appeals from both State Supreme Courts and Federal Courts of Appeals. One significant difference between the Supreme Court and lower federal courts in the United States, is its option *not* to hear a case that comes its way; this is called **appellate jurisdiction**. Of the thousands of cases sent to the Supreme Court annually, only a fraction of them are actually heard. For a case to be heard, at least four of the justices must agree on the need for the hearing.

When the Court agrees a particular case warrants a hearing, they will issue a ***writ of certiorari*** to the lower court from whence the case comes. The *writ of certiorari* compels the lower court to forward all documentation and records to the Supreme Court for review. If, after this review, the Supreme Court decides not to hear the case, they can dismiss the writ.

The Supreme Court serves in terms. A **term** of the Supreme Court lasts nearly ten months, from the first Monday of October until early in July. These terms are split up by **sittings** that allow for a certain number of cases to be heard as well as time for writing and issuing of opinions.

Supreme Court decisions are complex and very rarely unanimous. The majority rules in Supreme Court hearings and what the majority decides, becomes the ruling of the Court. One justice, who is a member of the majority, will write the findings of the Court in the official Opinion. The other agreeing justices will write *concurring opinions*, while those who disagree with the majority will write *dissenting opinions*.

STATE COURT HISTORY

Beginning much earlier than the organization of the federal court system were the state court systems. Our nation's founders had a bad taste in their mouth when coming from England. They were accustomed to the King controlling everything and wanted to be sure that the Federal government in their new land didn't have the same all-encompassing power. A dual Court system was developed that allowed states to create and interpret their own laws in a manner they saw fit as long as it was justifiable under the United States Constitution.

Originally, each of the original colonies had their own court system for settling criminal and civil matters. Prior to the American Revolution, these colonial court systems were disorganized and differed greatly. The early colony of Pennsylvania used a referee system where one individual, referred to as the "peacemaker," presided over criminal and civil matters. The belief was that every person could serve as their own legal counsel and represent their own interests in the best manner. This peacemaker would hear the dispute and his rulings would be binding. This referee system ended in 1766, but you can still see its effects today in States where magistrates are known as "justice of the peace."

One of the problems of early court systems was the distrust of attorneys. Corruption and abuse of power by attorneys was fresh in the colonists' minds and they did not want to trust attorneys after their negative experiences under the Crown in England. Early on, statutes were created that severely limited attorneys' rights to practice. Virginia had a law on the books that prohibited attorneys from collecting fees for their work. Other colonies strictly controlled the amount of authorized attorneys, or **barristers**, as they were also known. Controls were placed on the location and amount of schooling required for attorneys.

The original state courts that began to develop following the Revolution were quite disorganized. Many left no outlets for appeals and those who did would often have the appeal heard by the State Legislature. As time went on, however, the need for more courts and greater organization became obvious. The late 1800s brought a large population growth and the settlement of the frontier. This also brought with it an increase in both civil and criminal disputes. State Legislatures saw this increased need and began establishing more organized systems.

STATE COURT ORGANIZATION

Although the states were free to reorganize their court systems in any way they wanted, many followed a model of the federal courts and made a three-tier system. Others, however, did not and continued to have smaller courts with specific and limited jurisdiction on certain cases. For years, a move to join all state court systems under similar organizational models has been under way. Beginning in the early 1900s and continuing today, the simplification and organization of state courts systems has been a struggle. Some states readily embraced the proposed streamlined organizational models, while others are resistant to change.

Those courts following the federal model organized their system into a three-tiered approach. These tiers included:

1. Trial courts with limited jurisdiction (lower courts)
2. Trial courts with general jurisdiction (higher courts)
3. Appellate courts

Despite the three-tiered federal model, additional specialized and local courts abounded. Traffic courts and drug courts are examples of those we see commonly today. Problems associated with disorganization and multiple specialized courts include overlapping jurisdictions, among others.

STATE TRIAL COURTS

Criminal court matters begin in the trial courts. Courts of **limited jurisdiction**, often referred to as lower courts, typically hear minor cases including misdemeanors, infractions, and small civil claims. They may be the first stop for a felony charge but will only handle the arraignment or first appearance, bail setting, and the task of taking pleas. These lower courts are far more informal and personal. They will typically handle a multitude of cases on a daily basis.

High courts, or courts of **general jurisdiction**, can hear any criminal case. These courts are referred to as high courts, superior courts, or circuit courts, depending on the particular state's system. In addition to hearing criminal cases, they may serve as the first avenue of appeals for judgments issued in the lower courts of limited jurisdiction. In cases of appeal, the defendant may be entitled to a **trial *de novo***, or a completely new trial under the circuit court, rather than just a review of the original hearing.

STATE APPEALS COURTS

States typically have more than one type of appeals courts. They usually have both the courts of appeals as well as the state supreme court. While all states have a supreme court, not all states have an intermediate appellate court. With appeals such as this, a new trial is not granted but the facts and findings of the prior hearing are reviewed by the higher court. The records of the prior hearing are reviewed to be sure that the process was carried out fairly and in accordance with state law and procedure.

The majority of lower courts' decisions are affirmed on appeal. However, sometimes circumstances exist where the appeal is won and the prior decision is overturned. When this happens, the case may be sent back to the lower court for a re-trial. In states where there is both an intermediate appeals court and a supreme court, the case can be appealed from trial court, to appeals court, and then onto the state supreme court. If either party is still dissatisfied with the results, they can then attempt to be granted a review by the U.S. Supreme Court.

ADULT COURT SYSTEMS

In the United States, adult courts systems and proceedings are **adversarial** in nature. This means that there are two sides, the State and the defendant, facing off in an effort to defend their interests. This doesn't mean that no-holds-barred arguing ensues but that the adversarial system is organized and controlled by procedural rules laid out in statutes and practiced through years of tradition.

The right to be presumed innocent means that the burden of proof rests with the state. It is not up to the defendant to prove she didn't commit a crime, but it is up to the prosecution to prove that she did, *beyond a reasonable doubt*. "Beyond a reasonable doubt" is referred to as the standard of proof in criminal courts. This means that if the defense can show that there is reasonable doubt that the defendant committed the offense; the defendant must be found not guilty.

There are typical acts in all adult court proceedings. The prosecutor acts on behalf of the state in attempting to prove a violation of law has taken place. The defense attorney acts on behalf of her client, attempting to prove reasonable doubt exists. The judge watches all of this and ensures that each side is adhering to those procedural rules. In a jury trial, the jury determines guilt or innocence and recommends a sentence to the judge.

COURT PROCEEDINGS

Arraignment

The journey to trial can be long and arduous. It all begins with the first appearance in front of the judge. The first appearance, referred to as an **arraignment**, is where the defendant's charges will be read and he may have the opportunity to enter a plea if he so chooses. Typically, no evidence can be submitted at the arraignment. It is also at the arraignment that the judge will inform the defendant of some of his basic rights including the right to counsel. At the arraignment, the judge will determine if the defendant needs and wants a court-appointed attorney.

Another basic right usually explained at arraignment is the **right to a trial by jury**, as granted in the Sixth Amendment, in all felony and some misdemeanor cases. Not all trials are jury trials. If a defendant so chooses, he can elect to have a **bench trial** or one where the judge determines guilt or innocence.

If it is a felony charge, a date may be set for a preliminary hearing. In some states preliminary hearings are also available for more serious misdemeanors. However, in most circumstances, misdemeanors will move directly to a trial date (assuming the defendant doesn't plead guilty at arraignment). Also, under some circumstances a defendant can waive his right to a preliminary hearing and the case will move directly to trial. It is also at the arraignment that the judge may decide to set bail.

Pleas

Pleading "guilty" or "not guilty" aren't the only options for defendants. Most states allow for a no contest or *nolo contendere* plea. By pleading no contest, the defendant is not admitting guilt but stating they will not fight the charges. Although this is not taken by the court as an admission of guilt, it does require that the defendant face the same sentencing range that someone who was convicted would face.

Bail

Bail refers to a cash amount the defendant needs to pay to the court in order to be released prior to trial. If the defendant fails to appear at future court dates, the bail is often forfeited and applied to fees and fines. A **bond**, however, is a promise to appear at future court proceedings. Bond will take the form of cash or property and often as a 10% assurity bond. This means that only 10% of the total bond is due at the immediate time. Occasionally, in the case of minor offenses a defendant may be released on their own **recognizance**. This simply means that the judge is taking the defendant's word that he will return to court, but not requiring monetary collateral.

Bail and bond are typically only available when the judge can determine that the defendant is not a risk to society or himself and that he is not a **flight risk**, meaning he will return for future court dates. Some serious felonies are not eligible for bail, but those vary by state.

Preliminary Hearing

If the defendant chooses to exercise his right to a preliminary hearing, that date may be set at arraignment. The **preliminary hearing** is similar in style to a trial, but it is not there to establish guilt or innocence. It requires the prosecution (the state) to show to the judge that only probable cause exists to send the case to trial. **Probable cause** does not mean the state has to prove the defendant's guilt, merely that there is enough evidence that a reasonable person could believe the defendant committed the crime.

At the preliminary hearing both the prosecution and defense are allowed to present evidence. If the judge determines enough evidence exists, he may set a trial date at that time. If probable cause does not exist, the charges may be dropped.

Getting Ready for Trial

Waiting for a trial to happen can be an exercise in patience. It is not out of the question for a trial to take place one year or more after the initial arrest. This period can be filled with continuance after continuance. A **continuance** is a request, by either the prosecution or defense, for an extension prior to trial. Perhaps one of the sides needs more time to prepare or there may be scheduling conflicts.

Also, prior to trial, a jury must be selected. In a process called **voir dire**, the prosecutor and defense attorney slowly work through a large pool of potential jurors until the panel is selected. Voir dire allows the attorneys to dismiss potential jurors who may be biased about the trial at hand. The adversarial attorneys use challenges to remove people they do not want serving on the jury. There are three types of challenges used in jury selection.

1. Challenges to the array: when one side believes that the pool is not representative of the community or that it is biased.

2. Challenges for cause: make the argument that a specific juror may be biased or impartial.

3. Peremptory Challenges: removal of a potential juror without having to show cause. These are used often when the person may not implicitly state they are biased but the prosecution or defense believes they may have deep-seated biases. However, as stated, there is no requirement for the attorney to give a reason when making a peremptory challenge.

Plea Bargaining

Plea bargaining can occur at nearly any stage in the criminal trial process. Typically though, it happens in preparation for trial. A **plea bargain** is where the prosecution lowers the charge in exchange for a guilty plea. The prosecution may offer a plea bargain to the defendant for a variety of reasons. Perhaps they are concerned they will not have enough evidence to get a conviction at trial. By offering the defendant a "plea deal" they can ensure her conviction, without having to go to trial. The defense may agree to a plea because they are leery of their chances at trial or the defendant does not want to face the longer sentence.

It is important to note that a judge is not bound by a plea agreement. While the prosecution will likely offer a sentencing recommendation to the judge that the defendant would find acceptable, the judge is not required to follow this recommendation. That having been said, judges are typically accommodating to sentence recommendations when plea agreements are in place.

Trial

Once trial has finally arrived, the two sides will argue their case in front of the judge and jury (in jury trials). Trials typically follow a specific schedule similar to this:

1. Opening Statements
2. Presentation of Evidence
3. Closing Arguments

4. Judge's Instructions to the Jury
5. Jury Deliberations
6. Verdict

Opening Statements

The trial begins with opening statements from the prosecution. These opening statements are an introduction to the trial. At this time the prosecuting attorney will tell the jury what they intend to prove and describe how they will show the defendant's guilt. Once the prosecution is done, the defense can also share opening statements with the jury. The defense attorney, should they choose to make opening statements, will tell the jury how they intend to dispute the charges. Sometimes the defense will decide not to make opening statements and the trial will move to the presentation of evidence.

Presentation of Evidence

The presentation of evidence is the meat of the trial. This is where both sides argue their case. The prosecution tries to prove "beyond a reasonable doubt" that the defendant is guilty. The defense works on his behalf to show the jury that he is innocent of the charges.

Evidence can be anything deemed useful to a judge or jury in deciding the facts of the case. It can be in the form of physical evidence, witnesses and expert testimony, photographs, written documents, or videos. **Direct evidence** refers to evidence that directly proves a fact. This could be video documentation or eyewitness testimony. **Circumstantial evidence** is evidence that requires interpretation or requires the jury to reach their own conclusion. The majority of evidence presented in criminal trials is circumstantial.

The judge closely watches the presentation of evidence to be sure that all procedural rules are followed and jurors are not misled. One of the greatest tasks a judge has at trial is determining what evidence is submissable and what evidence is irrelevant. For instance, in the last 20 years judges have begun questioning the use of a woman's sexual history as admissible evidence in rape trials. The argument is that her sexual history is irrelevant to the rape.

Witness testimony carries a lot of weight at trial and much of the evidence submitted is witness testimony. When referring to trial, **testimony** is spoken evidence given under oath. Witnesses can be police officers, eyewitnesses, victims, and even the defendant. The Fifth Amendment protects potential defendants when it grants the right to remain silence and to avoid self incrimination.

In the 1965 case, *Griffin v. California*, it was determined that when a defendant invoked her Fifth Amendment right, it could not be treated as an admission of guilt. Prior to this decision, defendants who refused to testify were often attacked by the prosecution and therefore perceived as guilty by the jury. However, sometimes it may be in the best interest of the defendant's case for her to testify. This is a decision for the defense to make.

As every witness is presented, both sides will have the opportunity to question them. The defense must keep this in mind when deciding whether or not to let the defendant testify at her own trial. When a witness is first introduced, the introducing party can conduct *direct examination*. Direct examination is followed by *cross-examination* from the other side. After cross examination, the party who introduced the witness has another opportunity to *redirect examination*. Following redirect examination, the secondary side can again cross examine, referred to as *recross-examination*. This process of examination and cross examination can go back and forth until both parties are satisfied.

Important to note is the concept of **hearsay**. Heresy refers to something that isn't based on the personal knowledge of the witness. What this means is that witnesses who testify on what they *heard* happened, or if they do not have direct knowledge, will likely have their testimony questioned by the opposing side. Hearsay is traditionally not allowed to be admissible in court. Occasionally if someone with firsthand knowledge is unable to testify, an exception will be made.

Closing Arguments

This is the conclusion of the adversarial process. Both the prosecution and defense will have one last opportunity to sum up their case for the jury or judge. This is often the dramatic scene in television and movies where the attorneys save their best for last. This is the final chance they have to sway the jury in their favor. Who gets to go first in closing arguments depends on the state.

Judge's Charge to the Jury
Prior to the jury deliberations, the judge will give them clear instructions. Although specific wording varies from jurisdiction to jurisdiction, all judges remind the jury of their duty to objectively consider all of the evidence. They will also be reminded of the elements of the statute that the defendant is accused of violating.

Some states allow the judge to voice his opinion over certain evidence and witnesses at this time, while others only permit the judge to objectively review the evidence. Once the charge has been given, the jury will be removed from the courtroom to begin deliberations.

Jury Deliberations

Sometimes jury deliberations last a matter of minutes. In other cases, jury deliberations can go on for days. Some states require the jury to reach a unanimous decision. The U.S. Supreme Court has ruled that this is only necessary in capital murder cases. A jury that is required to come to a unanimous decision can easily become deadlocked when one dissenter holds their ground and refuses to join the opinion of the majority. In some states this is grounds for a retrial, while in others the judge will simply attempt to give the jurors a pep talk by recharging them. Once a verdict is reached, that verdict is delivered to the judge. A conviction leads to sentencing while an acquittal marks the end of the journey for a freed defendant.

Sentencing

Depending on the conviction, the defendant may be waiting in jail until the sentencing date. Most often the judge will set the sentencing date directly after announcing the verdict. Sometimes the defendant will be sentenced the same day.

How does a judge decide on the sentence?

When it comes time for the judge to sentence, he will take several things into consideration. One of the greatest determining factors of the sentence will be the crime of which the defendant was convicted.

A **pre-sentence investigation** will likely be ordered by the court to assist the judge in sentencing. This extensive background investigation and report are usually completed by probation officers in the jurisdiction of the court.

The pre-sentence report will include everything from the defendant's past criminal history, employment record, family situation, and present living environment. The judge looks at this information to determine which sentence is appropriate for that defendant. The reporting officer usually makes a recommendation to the Court. If he sees instability and unemployment, probation may not be a good risk. However, if the defendant has a solid work history and strong family support, she might be a good candidate for such a suspended sentence.

If there is a victim that wishes to speak or have a statement read at sentencing, the judge will also take that into consideration. A **victim impact statement** can detail how the crime has affected the victim and describe any changes in her life as a result of the crime. This victim impact statement shows the human side to the crime.

If the victim is no longer alive, family members can give victim impact statements.
There are two sentencing models used in the United States; determinate and indeterminate sentencing have both been hailed as the right way to sentence at different points in time. This is because they both have redeeming and negative qualities.

Allocution refers to when, during or just prior to sentencing, a judge gives the defendant a chance to speak on their own behalf. The defendant is not sworn in and what they say is not subject to cross examination. Typically, allocution serves one of two purposes. The defendant may be accepting a plea bargain which requires them to publicly admit to guilt, in which case this is when they would do so. The second purpose is in an attempt to sway a judge or jury with a personal appeal before they make their decision.

Indeterminate sentencing is the sentencing model that encourages rehabilitation of offenders and judicial discretion. It does this through relatively unspecific sentences. For instance, a judge has two offenders, both convicted of robbery. One has a history of violence and instability. The other offender may have been an average citizen with strong community ties and a stable history. Indeterminate sentences allow judges to weigh the different circumstances surrounding a case and sentence accordingly.

Indeterminate sentencing encourages rehabilitation by promoting good behavior on active prison sentences through earning **good time**. Good time is an amount of time deducted from an offender's sentence after a certain period of incarceration dependant on their good behavior, but sometimes awarded automatically.

Determinate Sentencing came about due to the abuse of judicial discretion. With great power comes great risk, and indeterminate sentencing brought about many allegations of judicial prejudices and bias. Couple that with the variation in judges' personal philosophies (one judge might be known as lenient and the other as the "hanging judge"), and you are asking for problems. To remedy this, some states have moved toward a determinate model.

Determinate sentencing, also referred to a fixed or presumptive sentencing, sets one punishment for each offense. For example, everyone convicted of assault in the first degree would be sentenced to the same prison term. While determinate sentencing does limit judicial bias and extreme differences between judges, it also does not allow for important factors surrounding the case to be taken into consideration at sentencing.

Some variances on determinate sentencing include states that require the judge to sentence within a limited range for each crime. Others may allow the judge to consider *aggravating* and *mitigating* circumstances in considering a slight stray from the presumptive sentence.

Federal Sentencing Guidelines, an example of determinate sentencing, may be followed by the judge. These guidelines were originally mandates by the federal government created to specify exact sentences for crimes. In 2005 the Supreme Court ruled those guidelines unconstitutional as mandatory and they have since become an optional recommendation rather than the rule.

Aggravating circumstances refer to those elements of a crime or offender's background that may result in the judge considering a harsher sentence than what is called for by the sentencing guidelines. **Mitigating circumstances**, however, refer to those circumstances that may sway the judge to impose a slightly lesser sentence than recommended by the guidelines.

One large critique of the determinant model is that it gives a lot of power to the prosecuting attorney. By taking away judicial discretion we allow the prosecution to, in an indirect way; determine the sentence by determining the charge. This may give the prosecutor more power than the judge in sentencing under the determinate model.

Also, a negative point to the determinate model is its failure to encourage good behavior behind bars. If offenders are not given incentive to act according to the rules, then what do they have to lose by breaking them.

Indeterminate sentencing takes away judicial discretion and, some say, discredits the profession of the judiciary. Judges are put in their position because of their unbiased application of the law. Proponents of this idea argue that the focus should be on a better screening of judges for slight biases rather than trying to prevent them from carrying out their duties.

JUVENILE COURT SYSTEMS

Although it varies slightly from state to state, the majority of states define the jurisdiction of the juvenile court system as children who have not yet turned eighteen, while some consider the determining age to be sixteen or seventeen.

A juvenile's entrance to the system begins with their arrest and the filing of a juvenile petition; this stage is referred to as the **intake**. The **juvenile petition** is a document taken out in juvenile court alleging the child is delinquent or in other ways in need of court intervention. Juvenile petitions are filed by family members, law enforcement, a teacher, neighbors or any other reputable member of the community. The majority of juvenile petitions are filed by law enforcement officers. You can think of a petition as the juvenile version of a criminal complaint.

Unlike the adult court system, detention for juveniles is avoided at all costs. In juvenile cases, **detention hearings** are typically held within 24 hours of apprehension to determine if holding the juvenile in custody is an absolute necessity. The detention hearing is presided over by a judge or juvenile intake officer. At this stage in the case, the presiding person can decide to hold the juvenile in custody, release them, drop the charges, or choose to divert the case. Diversion refers to sending the child to a job training program, drug treatment center, or another similar program.

The **preliminary hearing** may or may not be held in conjunction with the detention hearing. The preliminary hearing, in juvenile courts, allows the child and his parents to be informed of his rights and the procedure to follow. The judge will also look at the evidence and decide if probable cause exists for the case to move forward.

The child may also be diverted at this stage of the case. A **transfer hearing** may be held to determine if the case should be sent to adult criminal court where the juvenile will be charged as an adult. When determining if a case should be transferred, the court will take into consideration statutes applying to transfers and if the treatment resources available through the juvenile system would be sufficient for the child's needs.

The **adjudication hearing** is the "trial" of juvenile court. Due process rights for children are much like the rights for adults although some key differences exist:

1. Informal setting: The juvenile adjudication hearing is far less structured than the adult trial. The judge will have more of a fact-finding role in the juvenile court and the environment will be more relaxed.

2. No right to trial: Although some states provide juveniles with the right to trial, it is not guaranteed and the case of *McKeiver v. Pennsylvania* established that it was not guaranteed through the Constitution.

3. Privacy: For the sake of the juvenile, court proceedings are kept as private as possible.

4. Speed: Adjudication hearings are not the long drawn out procedures that adult trials are.

5. Philosophy and attitude of the court: Unlike in adult criminal cases, judges want to avoid the institutionalization of juveniles at all costs. This means that a court could make lenient rulings for the juvenile in an effort to increase his chances for rehabilitation.

Following the adjudication, a **disposition hearing** will take place as the final stage of the juvenile process. This is similar to sentencing in an adult court. The disposition hearing concludes with the **juvenile disposition** possibly recommending time in a juvenile correctional facility, a children's home, juvenile probation, or some other treatment.

CORRECTIONS

The purpose of corrections is to carry out and enforce sentencing from the criminal courts. Because of this it is important to examine the goals of sentencing and how they apply to corrections in the United States.

There are four generally accepted goals of sentencing. Each goal represents a sort of theory or sentencing philosophy. Each one examines different aspects of crime and criminological behavior. The four goals of sentencing are:

1. Deterrence
2. Rehabilitation
3. Retribution
4. Incapacitation

DETERRENCE

Deterrence refers to those actions that prevent people from committing future crimes. It deals with crimes that have not been committed yet. Deterrence is also an overall goal of the criminal justice system. When dealing with sentencing, however, it sentences offenders in order to serve as an example to others.

There are two distinctions made in deterrence. **General deterrence** is when a sentence serves as an example to deter others from committing the same crime. **Specific deterrence**, however, focuses on one individual and preventing *him* from further committing crimes. For example, if Joe Crime robs a liquor store, his sentence of five years in prison will hopefully deter others from robbing liquor stores (general deterrence) but will also deter Mr. Crime from robbing another liquor store (specific deterrence).

REHABILITATION

As a sentencing goal, rehabilitation attempts to bring about significant change in the behavior and mindset of offenders. It works through education and psychological treatment of the offender. Rehabilitation, as a sentencing goal for adults, is fairly new. It was used frequently in the sentencing of juveniles because it was believed that adults were either beyond repair, or that rehabilitation was somehow coddling the offender. As the popularity of psychology grew, so did the rehabilitation goal. It was not until the 1930s that sentencing reflected rehabilitative goals.

RETRIBUTION

As the earliest known reason for criminal punishment, retribution is the goal of vengeance. This is the "eye for an eye" goal. In modern days, the "**just deserts**" model of sentencing embraces retribution by stating that criminals *deserve* their punishment due to the acts that brought it on. It sees punishment for crimes as justified, deserved, and maybe even required.

Although some may view retribution as an archaic sentencing goal, it remains at the forefront anytime a tough-on-crime stance is taken by the public.

INCAPACITATION

Lastly, incapacitation seeks to protect society by removing the criminal's ability to commit future offenses. This is accomplished through both imprisonment and other controls that reduce the offender's ability to commit similar future crimes (i.e. chemical castration). The greatest example of incapacitation is the death penalty.

It is important to note that while retribution involves punishment, incapacitation only involves restraint. It is not unusual for an advocate of the incapacitation model to also be an advocate for kinder, gentler prisons.

It is obvious that not one single sentencing goal can be used independently. For this reason, corrections attempt to cover a multitude of these sentencing goals.

HISTORY

In early America there were no prisons. Local jails held petty criminals while serious crimes were usually punished by flogging, mutilation, hangings and exile. Although it was thought that these acts would deter, they certainly were retributive in nature and in some circumstances, incapacitating. That having been said, the death penalty was outlawed for a short period between the late 1600s and 1718 at the urging of Quaker William Penn (founder of Pennsylvania). In 1718, however, the colonies were ordered by the Throne to reinstate it.

Loosely following models of reform houses in England, Americans sought to build the first prisons. Two main models of prison organization arose. These were the Auburn system and the Pennsylvania system.

The **Auburn system**, developed in Auburn State Prison, New York in 1817, was often compared to slavery. The basic schedule of the Auburn System involved forced labor during the day, at which point the inmates would be all together, followed by solitary confinement at night. A strict silence was enforced at all times, and prisoners were transported in lockstep (the prisoners were in a close, single file line with one hand on the person in front of them and stepping in sync). The philosophy behind the Auburn system was that hard work in harsh conditions would not only deter and punish, but would also provide an avenue for the prison to pay for itself. Prisons under this model contracted with private industries for cheap labor, never paying the inmates.

The **Pennsylvania system** was quite contrary to the Auburn method. At Easter State Penitentiary in Cherry Hill, Pennsylvania, this model was developed. Inmates were confined to their solitary cell, 24 hours per day with only a Bible to read. Advocates of this model thought that this reflective time would allow for the offenders to come to great change.

Both prison systems were severely lacking in many areas. Both programs were responsible for many mental health problems in already unstable offenders. However, most early prisons leaned toward the Auburn system due to the financial benefits. These types of prisons whose intent was to capitalize on the free labor of inmates were referred to as **industrial prisons**.

Critics of the Auburn system won out when the Hawes-Cooper Act (1929) and the Amhurst Sumners Act (1935) severely restricted prison labor. Humanitarians were pleased that there wouldn't be slave labor in the prison systems and small business was pleased there wouldn't be an unattainable level of cheap competition. Out of this legislation sprouted what is known as the **state use system**, which only allows sale of products produced in prison to go to state offices. This includes furniture, cleaning supplies and license plates.

This industrial age of prisons led the way to what was known as the Punitive Era in the 1930s and early 1940s. This era was marked by a high value on retribution and a lack of educational and work programs. Inmates were simply put out of sight and out of mind. From the 1940s through the 1960s the United States prison systems went through an era of treatment offered through various means. The growing popularity of psychology coupled with a treatment model had the system believing in and encouraging good treatment and training for offenders. This era was marked by the **medical model** of corrections which held that all inmates were "ill" and in need of treatment. Individual therapy, group therapies and other psychological treatments proliferated behind prison walls.

The age of the medical model encouraged the belief that ex offenders could overcome their past and become effective members in the community. Because of this, the next era of corrections focused on community-based corrections. The need for treatment coupled with a new overcrowding problem led corrections officials to develop corrections that led away from traditional confinement and further depended on community programs and support. This is when halfway houses and work release programs became popular.

From the 1980s to the current time we have been experiencing an increasing problem of overcrowding in prisons. A large part of this is due to increased penalties for drug crimes created in the 1990s. Early on this huge overcrowding problem caused many within the system to give up hope of rehabilitating offenders. The **warehousing** strategy was one that attempted to discourage future recidivism by completely giving up on rehabilitation and instead focusing on incapacitation. (**Recidivism** refers to repetitious criminal behavior, or reoffending criminals.) Prisons are being built at an astronomical rate and they are being filled just as fast.

COMMUNITY CORRECTIONS

Community corrections are a sentencing option that is a movement away from traditional confinement in an effort to create correctional programs available within the community. Also known as community-based corrections, these include a variety of court-ordered programs and sanctions allowing offenders to remain in the community under some amount of supervision rather than serving time in a traditional prison.

PROBATION

One of the largest sectors of community corrections is the field of **probation**. Probation is a sentence served in the community while under some level of supervision by a probation officer. Many other community corrections options are also imposed as part of an offender's probation sentence. While an offender can be immediately sentenced to probation, most probationers are convicted, receive a sentence of active jail time, and immediately have that sentence *suspended* until completion of the probationary term. In most circumstances, if a probationer violates the terms of his probation, he will go back before a judge with the possibility of having that original jail sentence *activated*. Probation is not new and definitely not exclusive to the United States. With early probation in England (in the 1300s), a sentence could be "bound over for good behavior" and an offender would be released into the custody of a willing citizen.

Recognized as the first probation officer, John Augustus, a shoemaker from Boston, would attend court proceedings in his hometown and offer to take select offenders home with him as an alternative to imprisonment. When Augustus died in 1859, he was credited with taking over 2,000 offenders into his home to aid in their rehabilitation.

Conditions of Probation

Probation is no walk in the park and requires all offenders to abide by court-ordered conditions of the supervision. These conditions are categorized in one of two ways. Conditions that all probationers must abide by are referred to as **general conditions**. These vary from state to state but may include general instructions such as maintaining employment, obeying laws, not possessing firearms or frequenting establishments where alcohol is served. **Special conditions** however are those that are mandated for a specific offender by the judge. These conditions can include drug treatment and random urinalysis for drug offenders, or anger management classes and restraining orders for domestic offenders. These special conditions may be applied to all offenders who commit a certain crime or just to a specific offender that the judge feels is in need of them.

PAROLE

Parole is defined as the supervised release of offenders from confinement through the discretion of a paroling authority. Parole may be mandated through statute in certain situations, but is likely granted through a state's parole board after an offender has served a certain portion of their prison sentence. **Parole boards** serve to determine when an offender is ready for release and may also be responsible for determining if revocation of that release is necessary. Some states mandate a certain amount of re-entry parole (typically 60-90 days). Parole can be a way to ease the offender into living in the community; this can lessen the strain of **institutionalization**. Institutionalization refers to the mentality that becomes a part of the former inmate due to their time in prison. It can affect how they relate to people once they are released.

Parole Conditions

Parole conditions can be very similar to probationary conditions. Parolees typically sign an agreement prior to release promising to abide by the terms of their parole. Similar to probationers, parolees are also required to report in to a supervising officer. In some states officers supervise both probationers and parolees, while in some the role is specialized depending on the type of offender.

If a parolee is found to be in violation of the terms of his parole, he may go before the parole board or a judge with the potential outcome of being sent back to prison to serve the remainder of his sentence.

Pros/Cons

As with anything, there are positive aspects of the probation and parole systems as well as negative. However, you can see below that the positive aspects of probation and parole far outnumber the negatives. Some would argue that although they outnumber, they do not necessarily outweigh.

Pros	Cons
• **Restitution** can be paid while offenders are allowed to work and remain in the community. • The **cost** of community supervision is much less than institutional supervision. • Community and family **support** for a community offender is greater than for an inmate or ex-inmate. • Community supervision allows offenders to make greater use of **community resources**. • There is a much lower rate of **institutionalization**. • Offenders supervised within the community have better chances at true **rehabilitation**.	• Community supervision has a **lack of punishment**. • **Increased risk to the community**.

Legalities

Several Supreme Court decisions have affected the probation and parole systems as we know them.

Griffin v. Wisconsin (1987) ruled that probation and parole officers can search their offenders' residences without warrants or probable cause.

Mempa v. Rhay (1967) ruled that both notice and a hearing were required when revoking probation, overturning the prior case of *Escoe v. Zerbst* (1935). This hearing is called a **revocation hearing**.

Morrisey v. Brewer (1972) found that there was a need for safeguards in parole revocation hearings including: A) written notice of a hearing specifying the alleged violations, B) the need for evidence of the violation to be exposed, C) that the hearing authority must be neutral and detached, D) the offender has a chance to defend himself and E) cross-examine witnesses and F) that a written statement be provided to the offender summarizing the findings of the hearing.

Gagnon v. Scarpelli (1973) followed *Morrisey's* lead in extending many of those rights to probationers and also adding that probationers facing revocation were entitled to an attorney and that they were also entitled to two hearings, a preliminary hearing (to establish probable cause) and the more substantial revocation hearing.

Greenholtz v. Nebraska (1979) determined that it was not necessary for a parole board to divulge reasons for a denial of parole. This is not concerning revocation, but original granting of parole. It was decided that, although divulging this information could better prepare the offender for any future parole hearings, it was not necessary.

Bearden v. Georgia (1983) ruled that probation could not be revoked solely for failure to pay restitution and/or supervision fees if the failure was not intentional. For instance, Bearden could not pay his court ordered fees and restitution because he became unemployed through no fault of his own.

INTERMEDIATE SANCTIONS

Also referred to as alternative sanctions, intermediate sanctions refer to sanctions that fall in the middle, between the harsh incapacitation of imprisonment and probationary terms. Many intermediate sanctions can be used in conjunction with a term of probation as a probation condition. They can also be used independently. Intermediate sanctions are less expensive per offender, they have a less significant social cost by allowing citizens to remain with their families and employers, and they provide flexibility.

Intermediate sanctions include split sentences, shock probation and shock parole, shock incarceration, community service, intensive supervision, electronic monitoring, and boot camps, to name a few.

A **split sentence** is one that requires the convicted offender to serve a period of incarceration followed by a period of probation. This kind of sentencing is quite common and is often used for minor drug offenses. It serves as a warning to the early offender that with more law violations will come more incarceration.

Shock probation and shock parole allow a period of supervision after incarceration. Shock probation is a program which allows defendants who are sent to jail to receive probation within a short time of their imprisonment (less than six months). The idea behind shock probation is that for some criminals, a short time in jail is enough to "shock" them out of a criminal lifestyle. Typically the first few months in jail are considered to be the hardest for a person, whereas the longer they spend imprisoned the more they adjust to it, and they can even pick up additional criminal traits. The laws governing the granting of shock probation vary by state. Typically it is considered only for first time offenders for which a judge believes the chance of reform is high. The practice can be beneficial to both the state and the individual. It allows them to proceed with their lives sooner, and is reduces the cost to the state of holding them in jail.

Typically this is different from normal probation and parole supervision in that offenders must apply for the community supervision. Many of these offenders are not aware that they will be released early in circumstances like this.

Shock incarceration is primarily used on young first-time offenders in an effort to scare them straight. Boot camps are an example of shock incarceration. These systems provide highly structured militaristic programs. Offenders are typically only there for a short, intense amount of time.

Mixed Sentences are those that require some amount of incarceration sprinkled into a probation term. The offender may serve only weekends in jail, which allows her to maintain community ties and employment.

Growing in popularity is **electronic monitoring** or home confinement, also known as house arrest. **House arrest** is used as an intensive community supervision tool. It allows offenders to stay outside the prison system, but only within the confines of their home. Certain technologies also allow the probation officer to program in the offender's work hours and location, so if the offender does not immediately return home after work, the officer will be alerted to the violation.

Another possible sentence type is community incarceration, which is a type of probationary status in which the defendant is not sent to jail, but they are monitored and must follow a set of instructions. For example, an individual placed on parole may be required to attend therapy, make routine check-ins or hold a job to avoid imprisonment.

Two contrasting theories in the field of criminal justice are those of retribution and restitution. These theories deal with the idea of imprisonment, and what its purpose is. The theory of retribution is the philosophy that criminals have violated a law and it is therefore the responsibility of law enforcement to place that person in jail. Restitution views imprisonment as the just punishment afforded to criminals. The criminal deserves to be jailed for breaking the law, in and of itself.

On the other hand, the theory of restitution takes the viewpoint that the commission of a crime was in fact infringing another individual's rights. Because it takes this viewpoint, the purpose of punishing a criminal is forcing them to make restitution. In other words, they have wronged an individual and need to find some way to compensate them for the damage that they inflicted.

PRISONS

With the constant growth in population comes the constant growth in crime. Our prison system is growing faster than the industry can keep up. According to the Bureau of Justice Statistics, in 2006 there were 501 sentenced inmates for every 100,000 American citizens. This equates to about 1 per 200. This figure is huge. One aspect that has changed over the past ten years is the offenses that are getting people prison time. In the 1980s and 1990s drug convictions accounted for much of the prison populations; this figure is beginning to see a decline as the criminal justice system focuses on **selective incapacitation**.

Selective incapacitation refers to the practice of only sentencing the most dangerous offenders to prison. This method of incapacitation reduces overcrowding and costs. Used in conjunction with community intermediate sentences, the system is still able to serve those offenders who were convicted of crimes considered not as serious.

Security Levels

Prisons are categorized by the level of security they provide. Some prisons may serve offenders of multiple security levels; those are then classified either by that determination or by the highest security level they are equipped to handle.

Minimum security institutions may not fit what you have pictured in your mind as an institution filled with offenders. Some of them appear similar to college campuses. Inmates are generally housed in dormitories, with many sharing a large room. Newer facilities may provide inmates with private rooms, allowing them to decorate their walls with photos and magazine clippings. The inmates typically have access to canteens (stores) where they can purchase toiletries and snacks. If there are fences, they are typically low and not electrified. These are facilities that may have work release and furlough programs. **Furloughs** are temporary passes that allow the inmate to leave the facility for a certain amount of time, from a few hours to a weekend.

Medium security prisons are plentiful and resemble maximum security prisons. It is not uncommon for a prison to be classified as medium-maximum. These institutions do not allow furloughs or work release and although the inmates have some privileges, the medium security prison does resemble what you may see in the movies. In this level of security, inmates may be allowed to roam the "yard" freely. The yard refers to the outside area used for recreation in a prison. They may also have access to the canteen and be able to hang photos in their cells. Some of the housing may be dormitory in style, but typically inmates are in cells and dormitories would only be used as an effort to combat overcrowding. The prison is surrounded by barbed and electrified fences and, oftentimes, armed guards.

Most largely populated states only have a few maximum security prisons. These are for offenders who need higher levels of security. They bear a resemblance to medium security prisons but traffic is more controlled and privileges are fewer. Inmates are housed in one- or two-man cells and the amount of property they are allowed to have is much more controlled. A practice also conducted in medium security prisons, "counts" are taken throughout the day to account for all of the inmates. The prison is surrounded by high fences and walls and they have armed guards watching from towers. Also within the prison walls are separate housing areas for inmates who need special control.

Supermax prisons are much fewer in number and much tighter in security. These inmates are the most dangerous in the country and are sent to these prisons because these facilities are equipped to handle them. Most of the time these prisons are only comprised of single cells. They resemble segregation cells in that they are small and stark. Property is extremely limited in these prisons. Staff-to-inmate ratios are much higher but direct staff-to-inmate contact is much lower. When possible, inmates are kept out of reach of staff through the use of plexiglass walls and small slots to pass materials and lock/unlock handcuffs.

Disciplinary Procedures

Prison is filled with criminals. Some of these criminals continue to commit crimes while behind bars. From committing assaults, participating in gangs, and competing in the illegal drug trade, the criminal life inside of prison reflects life outside the prison. Luckily when an inmate violates the rules of the institution there is a disciplinary process in place.

In most prisons, a rule violation warrants a "write up." This is sort of a ticket citing the offender of the rule violation and putting administration on notice that a rule has been violated. The inmate will go before a disciplinary committee to answer to the charges. Unlike a court of law, disciplinary procedures within the walls are very informal and rely on the judgment of those professionals making up the board. If the inmate is found guilty of the charge, he may be sanctioned to extra work duty, cell restriction (sort of a house arrest for inmates), visitation limitations, phone restriction, or segregation.

There are two types of segregation. Many prisons have several segregation statuses, but we will look at two of the most common. **Disciplinary segregation** typically refers to a temporary segregation status put on the inmate immediately following a serious rule violation. The inmate may be put in disciplinary segregation to ensure the safety of the institution until the disciplinary board can hear his "case." Disciplinary segregation can also be used as a consequence after the disciplinary hearing. This is mainly used to teach the inmate a lesson, as punishment. Inmates typically don't spend long lengths of time in disciplinary segregation.

Administrative segregation, however, can be a longer imposition of solitary. Administrative segregation is used when the inmate has shown himself to be a constant risk to the security of the institution. These people may have a history of attacking other inmates, or even staff. They may be key leaders in the prison drug trade, or a gang kingpin on the prison yard. These inmates are the most dangerous.

When an inmate is placed in administrative segregation, often referred to as ad. seg., he will be given a review date. Periodically he will meet with a review board to see how he is functioning in the severely restricted status. This board is often made up of high level custody staff, mental health personnel and even the warden. These segregation reviews are in place to monitor the inmate's well being. Unlike disciplinary segregation, ad seg can be a long term confinement. If an inmate cannot be trusted to be placed in general population, he will be closely supervised in administrative segregation.

Segregation status brings with it several sanctions. Inmates who are used to showering every day and visiting the yard for recreation will be seriously restricted. They may only be able to shower three times a week and go outside for one hour, three times a week. This "yard time" will be spent in a solitary yard, limiting contact with other inmates and staff. Property will be restricted, as will visitation and phone privileges.

Prison Populations

A look at who is filling the prisons yields some interesting results. In 2006, according to the Bureau of Justice Statistics, 2,258,983 inmates filled the nation's prisons. Approximately 50% of those offenders were serving time for violent crimes. Other inmates were convicted of drug crimes (20%), property crimes (20%), and crimes against the public order (<10%).

Although over time the number of correctional facilities in the United States has been increasing, so has the number of individuals occupying them. According to the Bureau of Justice statistics, the ratio of inmates to correctional officers in federal prisons rose from 9.0 to 10.3 between 2000 and 2005. In state prisons the numbers are slightly more favorable with a rise from 4.6 to 4.9 in the same ratio.

One of the most interesting ways to evaluate prison population statistics is by looking at race. Ignoring racial sentencing disparities would be a blatant disregard for an obvious problem. In 2006, according to the Bureau of Justice Statistics one white American man was incarcerated per 205. With Hispanic Americans that number was one in 79. With African Americans, that number was 1 in 32. A quick answer to this obvious disparity would be that African American men are committing more crime than white Americans. While this may be somewhat true, there are many factors that play into this. Judicial sentencing disparities still exist in this country and a convict of color is likely to get a longer sentence than other offenders. Also, looking at several criminological theories, we can see potential reasons for the disparity as well. In particular, the conflict theory, which states that poverty-stricken citizens will break the law in order to achieve those things that are so coveted in America. With minority populations higher in the lower economic class you can't help but determine that a greater lack of opportunities exists.

The national average is about one guard to six inmates, which fluctuates based on the security level of the prison.

Female offenders are also on the rise. In 2006 the amount of women in prison grew 4.5% while the population of male inmates only grew 2.7%. In the past women inmates had typically been convicted of property crimes or drug violations. Now, however, more and more women are committing violent crimes, increasing the need for more secure female prisons.

There are many problems faced by incarcerated individuals, but there is a set of problems which tend to be more prevalent among or specific to female inmates. For example, certain health care issues such as pregnancy affect an estimated 7-10 percent of female inmates, with the trend rising over time. Ensuring that they receive adequate care throughout pregnancy and childbirth is a challenge because prisons are not equipped for it. Following the birth is the challenge of determining what to do with the baby. If the mother wants to keep the baby, it creates difficulties determining how to proceed. It is generally accepted that the first year is pivotal in a mother/child relationship.

Another huge issue faced by female prisoners is motherhood. Statistics show that around two thirds of incarcerated women have children under the age of 18 – having anywhere from one to more than five children. This introduces an additional set of problems such as arranging visitation. Although regular visits are encouraged, the fact that there are fewer female prisons than male prisons means that women are typically held farther from their children.

CAPITAL PUNISHMENT

The death penalty is the ultimate in sanctions. It has been around for a very long time, but has gone through several changes in the United States. Biblical Israel used stoning as the execution of choice. Romans typically used beheading, burning, and even feeding some to the lions. During the Dark Ages, execution was commonplace and carried out in a methodical fashion. Offenders were crushed with huge stones, dumped in boiling oil, and thrown into fire. The thought at this time was that if the criminal were truly innocent, God would intervene and save them from their fate. This was referred to as **trial by ordeal** and used quite readily.

In early America, hanging was the preferred method of execution. It was inexpensive and efficient. By the late 1800s, electrocution replaced hanging. As the last State whose *sole* execution method was by electric chair, the Nebraska Supreme Court recently (Feb. 2008) ruled that it constituted cruel and unusual punishment. Currently, lethal injection is the method of choice in the United States.

Not all crimes mandate the death penalty. Those crimes that carry a potential death sentence are referred to as **capital offenses**. Most capital offenses involve the murder of another person. According to the Bureau of Justice Statistics, in 2007, 42 people were executed in the United States. Twenty-six of these executions occurred in Texas. Forty-one of the 42 executions were carried out through lethal injection. Law concerning the death penalty is ever evolving. This country has gone through several periods when the death penalty was abolished, from colonial days until a de facto moratorium lasting from 1967 through 1977.

ISSUES AND TRENDS IN CORRECTIONS

Drugs in Prison

The introduction of controlled substances is something that plagues America's prisons every day. While contraband alcohol, referred to as hooch, can be made by inmates within the walls, illegal drugs are brought in from the "outside." Any drug that can be purchased in the community can typically be purchased on a prison yard.

Drugs and hooch in prison can make inmates more aggressive and uncontrollable. Typically, inmates who are in need of physical control can be contained with strategically implemented defense moves performed by staff. However, if under the influence of drugs or highly concentrated alcohol, an inmate may feel no pain and be virtually unstoppable. Another risk is health-related illness. If an inmate becomes sick due to drug usage or overdose, finding out what caused the illness in order to properly remedy it can be nearly impossible.

The prison drug trade has a serious impact in the dynamics of prison life. When a certain group of inmates control the drug trade, they control the hierarchy on the yard. The most physically powerful inmate in the prison may not be the most feared.

In an effort to control the prison drug trade, administrators must figure out where the drugs are coming from. The knee jerk reaction is that illegal substances are coming in at visitation time. A percentage of the controlled substances are brought in by visitors. By searching all visitors, administrators prevent some of this. However, visitors and inmates have perfected this skill over years and years of trial and error. Drugs can be hidden underneath clothing or in the body. Typically inmates are searched both entering visits and after visits in an effort to recover any contraband passed during visits, but still some get by.

More likely than visitation, sadly, is that the contraband is being brought in by staff. All prison staff is vulnerable to inmate games and the lure of easy money. Inmates will offer lucrative sums of money for staff to bring in small amounts of drugs and even tobacco (in tobacco-free institutions). An ongoing problem in correctional institutions is the revolving door of staff, many of them leaving due to corruptive acts.

Staff are trained to deal with the lure of corruption and taught all of the games that inmates may play. But, staff is new to the prison, while inmates have had years to perfect their manipulation. In an effort to control staff corruption, many states have implemented criminal charges for institutional staff that bring contraband into the facility.

Prison Gangs

Directly related to the prison drug trade are prison gangs. Many of the gang problems we see on the news as happening in the street, are related to issues behind the prison walls. Many street gangs began as prison gangs. Prison gangs are typically divided along racial lines. Riots and large violent acts in prison are often a result of gang activities. Many inmates in the larger prisons say that aligning yourself with a gang is necessary for self protection.

One problem with controlling the criminal acts of prison gangs can be ignorance on the part of administration and prison staff. Gang members will not communicate what is going on with prison staff. If a gang member is assaulted by a member of another gang, he will more than likely face segregation time rather than "snitch" on the offender. He will allow his fellow gang members to solve the problem with revenge rather than allow prison officials to handle it.

AIDS

AIDS and other deadly communicable diseases are an issue in prison as well. A subject not often broached is that of inmate sex. Although sexual contact between inmates is against the rules, it does happen. All sexual relationships in prison are potentially dangerous. The prison system administration faces a dilemma in that although they know the risks exist, giving inmates access to condoms would be perpetuating a violation of the rules. Also present is the security risk that HIV positive inmates may pose. If an inmate is discovered (by other inmates) to be infected with the virus, he may face being ostracized or even fall victim to violence from the other inmates.

Special Populations

While all inmates are in need of some level of help, be it counseling, education, or job training, many are in need of greater supports within the walls of prison. With the baby boomer generation getting older, the prison population is also getting older. Having a large number of inmates with the typical ailments of the elderly can put a strain on some prisons' limited medical facilities. This population has also put financial strains on the system as the state is responsible for medical costs (in most situations) when offenders are incarcerated. This growth of elderly inmates is called the "graying" of the prison system.

Mental health puts inmates and staff at risk in prisons as well. In the past, mentally ill inmates were often kept at separate institutions that did sort of a double duty as mental hospitals/prisons. Now however, due to overcrowding and simplification of the system, oftentimes the mentally ill are housed in normal prisons with the general population. This makes it difficult as the relationship between mentally ill inmates and staff, as well as other inmates, is a fragile one.

Mentally ill inmates may have gone undiagnosed at the time of trial or may have worsened since their conviction. Many inmates deal with a higher level of mental health problems once incarcerated. Medicating these inmates is one way to keep the most dangerous of them under control. In the Supreme Court case, *Washington State v. Harper* (1990), it was ruled that mentally ill inmates could be required to take drugs to assist in their control. If not taken willingly, then the drugs could be forcefully administered with a court order.

JUVENILE CORRECTIONS

A juvenile delinquent is a minor (a person under 18) who has committed a crime, but because of their age are not legally held responsible. Depending on individual situations, a juvenile may be tried as an adult for severe crimes, but in most cases legal systems have a separate set of rules for dealing with juvenile crimes. For example, there are separate juvenile detention centers and juvenile courts. Juvenile delinquency can occur in the form of virtually any type of crime, ranging from more serious violent crimes, to simple status offenses. Juvenile delinquency is of great concern because it is one of the fastest growing areas of crime, and increasing numbers of youth are involved in crimes at younger ages.

As previously discussed, juvenile detention is a last resort in the world of juvenile criminal procedures. However, those juveniles who are at a heightened risk to reoffend may be placed in a secure juvenile setting. These can be in the form of youth centers or detention facilities. Oftentimes, these facilities appear similar to high school campuses in an effort to reduce the likelihood of institutionalization of the youth. These facilities are purely rehabilitative in nature and focus on teaching the juveniles better ways of dealing with the difficult issues in their lives.

In an effort to keep juveniles out of these facilities, however, many alternatives exist. Youth homes in the community provide structure in a rehabilitative setting, allowing the child to experience the benefits of rehabilitation without being taken out of society. Juveniles may also be sentenced to juvenile probation with many of the same or similar probationary terms as adult offenders. Typically states have officers exclusively trained to handle juvenile probationers. These officers develop positive relationships with parents as well as administrators within schools and treatment programs.

With the growing number of juvenile offenders, legislators are in a race to stay ahead of the looming problems. The focus is on keeping these children out of the adult criminal world and if they succeed in rehabilitation early on, this goal might be achieved.

Status offenses are crimes which can only be committed by a certain classification (or status) of people. The term is generally applied to crimes which are committed by minors. For example, drinking alcohol, truancy, possession of a firearm and purchasing cigarettes are all exclusively juvenile crimes because they are only a crime when committed by a juvenile, and are otherwise legal. In some cases, a distinction is made between juvenile status offenders, who have committed crimes that are status offenses, and juvenile delinquents, who have committed crimes that are always illegal.

 Police

HISTORY AND ORGANIZATION

We are accustomed to viewing the police in a certain way. We see them in their uniforms, patrol cars, or even as the undercover agents we see on TV. However, the history of the police as we know them goes back to an age of minimal organization and more brute than brains.

Some of the first known police officers were in ancient Egypt. Little is known about these ancient police, but we do know that the pharaoh had public officers performing police functions. They carried a weapon made of a staff topped by a large metal knob. This may be where the baton, carried by police today, originated.

Taking their cue from the ancient Egyptians were the Greeks whose *ephori* were police, judge, and executioner, all in one. A body of five individuals, called an **ephor**, was elected annually to act as the main law enforcement. These ephori were given nearly unlimited powers and practiced a retribution-laden system. This system, with its limited numbers, lent itself quite readily to corruption.

In Rome, following the writing of the Twelve Tables, the emperor Augustus selected soldiers from his military to guard the palace and to patrol the city. Also established in Rome by Augustus were the **Vigiles**. The vigiles were initially fire fighters but later gained law enforcement responsibilities. They were a civilian force who sometimes ruled quite lawlessly. The term vigilante derives from the Vigeles. Another example of law enforcement in Rome were the **lictors**, who served as guards to the magistrates. The lictors would follow the direction of the magistrates from bringing criminals to the judge, down to carrying out executions.

Moving from ancient times to the middle ages in England, the **tithing** system was a self governing system in place to prevent the need for public law enforcement. Through the tithing system, communities kept themselves in line by forming organizational associations made up of similar people. If one person in the group committed a crime and was convicted, the entire group would be responsible for the imposed fine. The thought was that this sort of collective punishment would encourage self governing bodies, which were more reluctant to break laws.

The tithing was organized to contain ten families. Every man in the tithing would be a part of the police body. One member would be the head or a *chief tithingman* who would be responsible for duties similar to that of a mayor and judge. A group of ten tithings was referred to as a *reeve*, with one main chief over the reeve called a **shire-reeve**. The word sheriff is derived from the two Saxon words: "Scyre," county and "Reve" the Saxon word for keeper. The shire-reeve would spend his time traveling from reeve to reeve acting as head judge and police officer.

The tithing system established simple solutions to crime. Back then all they were looking to prevent were murder and theft. Crime at the time was not very developed. This community-based policing allowed every member of the tithing to get involved in crime prevention. If you, as a member of the tithing, saw a crime being committed, you would use the **Hue and Cry** method. Simply stated, you would shout for others to hear something similar to "Thief, stop!" Anyone who heard the hue and cry was then required to stop what they were doing and assist in the apprehension of the thief. Interestingly, the hue and cry was the predecessor to the citizen's arrest.

Once the criminal was apprehended, he would be brought before the chief tithingman who would make a judgment regarding his guilt and impose a punishment. Punishments at the time usually consisted of fines, restitution, or by working off the debt through servitude.

Even the concept of extradition finds its roots in the tithing system. If a criminal sought to hide himself in a neighboring village, the tithing he was in had an obligation to return the criminal to the tithing where the crime occurred to face punishment.

Another method used in the tithing system was when the shire-reeve called all able bodied men together to apprehend a criminal. This was referred to as the power of *posse comitatus*, and was the basis of what would later be referred to as a posse.

In 1066, England was invaded by William the Conqueror who made significant changes to the tithing system. He established military districts within England that were all headed by a *shire-reeve*. Each *shire-reeve* in the new system answered directly to the King. William also decided that the *shire-reeves* should *only* serve as a head of law enforcement, and selected judges to travel the country holding hearing and issuing sentences. This was the first separation of law enforcement and judicial roles.

Along with the new system, came new laws. William introduced laws establishing curfews and tax laws, as well as a book prescribing exact recommended sentences for particular violations. William the Conqueror's rule established the **Frankpledge** system, which referred to the guarantee of peace that each person gave the King. This system emphasized loyalty to the crown along with local community-level responsibility in maintaining peace.

Following his father's lead, King Henry I, the son of William the Conqueror, made additional strides in the development of law enforcement. His main contribution was called the **Leges Henrici**, which was a body of law that established certain crimes such as murder, robbery, and arson as being crimes against peace. This body set the significant precedence that there were certain laws that needed to be punished by the state and not by the community.

Watchmen and community patrols eventually evolved into police organizations much like what we see today. In the 1700s, local magistrate Henry Fielding was tired of the apathy shown by local police in response to crime waves overtaking London. He developed what would be called the **Bow Street Runners** after the street which he was a magistrate on. The Bow Street Runners soon became known as the best law enforcement officers in London. They were credited with taking down one of the most infamous crime leaders in London at the time.

What we know as modern day police, however, can be traced directly back to the London Metropolitan Police, developed in 1829 by Sir Robert Peel. The police force was revered as one of the best in the world and was made up of officers handpicked by Robert Peel. The officers became known as "bobbies" after their founder.

The Metropolitan Police saw two main precepts as key in law enforcement. First was that it was possible to discourage crime, and second, that regular patrol could prevent crime. Reception for the new force was not positive initially due to their heightened presence in the city. But once the people realized the positive effect of the ever present patrol, respect shifted.

AMERICAN POLICE HISTORY

The early American experience in law enforcement was similar to that of England in trying to find its way through new crimes and new needs for control. The American frontier provided a great hideout and vast area for criminals to settle. The frontier was referred to as "wild" not simply because of the wildlife, but also because of the lawlessness that prevailed. America's first vigilantes grew in the west frontier. Taking the law into their own hands, they tried to establish some kind of organization.

American cities were far from immune to crime in the early days. Starting with drafted citizens and moving to paid watchmen, the citizens of the cities wanted to be sure their new homes and lands were protected from the criminals who roamed the nights. American founders closely studied the London Metropolitan Police Force and the skills of its founder, Sir Robert Peel.

Paid watchmen, employed by the city, made up the first staff of the New York City Police Department in the early 1800s. Boston followed shortly after in 1855. By merging day and night watchmen forces, the early cities organized the first 24-hour police forces in America.

The early 1900s brought reform and further organization. The Fraternal Order of Police was organized and modeled after labor unions with the one key difference of prohibiting strikes in 1915. The development of technology such as automobiles, telephones and radios all deeply affected policing. Similar to today, new technologies further equipped police to deal with the ever evolving criminal mind.

WOMEN IN POLICING

Alice Stebbins Wells was the first female police officer on the LAPD. Previously a minister, after petitioning the mayor and authorities. She wanted to better serve the women and children that were victims of crime. She was sworn in September 12, 1910. She later started the International Policewomen's Association.

MODERN DAY POLICING

Today, police take all of the historic lessons and pair those with today's technologies to make policing a fine-tuned machine.

The Kansas City Preventative Patrol experiment was an experiment carried out in 1970 with the goal of determining the effect that the presence of a marked police car had on crime. The study specifically looked at the rates of crimes and the opinion of the public. The study found that having routine patrols carried out by marked police vehicles neither reduced the amount of crime that was occurring, nor did it have any effects on the public's general feeling of security. It concluded that resources should be allocated away from patrol problems and be placed where they could be more effectively used. The Kansas City Patrol experiment was also an important experiment because it demonstrated that there were ethical, effective and safe ways to carry out experiments relating to police work. Because the study experimented by contrasting patrols in marked and unmarked cars, the study both allowed officers to carry out their regular duties, and helped them to gain valuable information about police work.

Originally proposed by scientists James Wilson and George Kelling, the broken window theory describes a theory that the state of an urban area can affect crime levels. The idea behind the theory is that when people are around other people, they tend to conform to expectations and norms. However, if an individual is alone they can only rely on their surroundings. Therefore, well-kept surroundings will discourage crime because they speak to a higher level of standards. On the other hand, ill-kept surroundings, such as multiple broken windows and other problems, will indicate that a lower standard of respect and adherence to laws is tolerated, and that nobody cares.

POLICE ORGANIZATION

The United States has one of the most complex law enforcement systems in the world. Because we have police at the Federal, State, and local levels, it makes for a slew of different methods and organizational uniqueness.

FBI

At the Federal level, the FBI is the most well known (in both the country and quite possibly the world). The Federal Bureau of Investigation is tasked with living up to its reputation of pure professionalism and high standards. It started in 1908 when it was originally designed to serve as the investigative department of the US Department of Justice. It began as a small organization of only 35 agents and has developed into an agency including over 30,000 total employees, over 12,000 of them agents.

Today, the FBI deals with a multitude of areas. Enforcing Federal law is no small job. The FBI protects the United States against terrorist efforts, assists local and State law enforcement, enforces Federal laws, and focuses on white collar crime, gambling law violations, arson, civil rights violations, violent serial offenders, and offenses that involve technology.

The FBI uses and administers a large DNA database referred to as CODIS which stands for Combined DNA Index System.

DEA

The United States Drug Enforcement Agency does exactly what you might think. It enforces federal drug offenses. It was developed in 1914 with the Harrison Narcotic Act under President Woodrow Wilson. Initially it was not referred to as the DEA, but was merely a small branch within the Bureau of Internal Revenue. Early on, the Agency kept quite busy attempting to stay ahead of the opium trade in the 1920s. Later, the DEA moved onto the illegal drug trade with the Mafia and attempting to keep illegal narcotics under control.

The Drug Enforcement Agency as we know it today was finally created and given such title in 1970 with the passage of the Comprehensive Drug Abuse Prevention and Control Act in response to the appearance of designer drugs such as LSD and the continuing drug problems that plagued our country. Today the DEA is constantly expanding in an attempt to outpace the growth of the illegal sale, transportation, and use of illegal drugs.

What agency determines what drugs are illegal? The Food and Drug Administration, or FDA, is a regulatory agency which reports to the United States Department of Health and Human Services and employs over 11,000 people. It is the responsibility of the FDA to ensure public health and safety. They do this by monitoring many products which come into contact with people, and ensuring that they are safe, sanitary and properly labeled. Their influence extends from food, drugs and vaccines to cosmetics, blood transfusions and radioactive products. It is the responsibility of the FDA to determine the safety of drugs, and if they are unsafe they can label them as illegal. It is then the responsibility of the Drug Enforcement Administration (DEA) to prevent people from abusing it and regulate other matters related to its use.

U.S. MARSHALS SERVICE

The U.S. Marshals began over 200 years ago when our first president, George Washington, appointed thirteen marshals to provide the majority of federal law enforcement. Marshals served as a sort of liaison between the people and the federal government. Up until 1969, the Marshals were very loosely regulated, but it was then that they received agency status and thus came under close supervision.

Today U.S. Marshals are a branch of law enforcement acting under the Office of the Attorney General. They conduct prisoner transports, arrest and pursue fugitives, provide security in Federal courts, and are personal security for Federal judges and magistrates. The Marshal Service also executes Federal warrants and transports high profile inmates. They are also responsible for handling and processing assets seized under federal law. The witness protection program also falls under the U.S. Marshals.

The Federal Air Marshal Service (FAMS) is an agency which operates under the Department of Homeland Security. Its purpose is to ensure the safety of individuals in the United States traveling by plane by identifying and deterring hostile or terrorist acts which occur on planes. It is the job of Federal Air Marshals to blend in with other individuals on flights and watch for potential problems. They are highly specialized in close quarters self-defense, criminal behavior and are highly proficient with firearms.

Other Federal Law Enforcement agencies include: the Bureau of Alcohol, Tobacco and Firearms, Bureau of Immigration and Customs Enforcement, Coast Guard, Washington D.C. Metropolitan Police Department, U.S. Secret Service, U.S. Park Police, Department of Defense Criminal Investigative Division, and Postal Inspections Services.

STATE LAW ENFORCEMENT AGENCIES

State law enforcement agencies began cropping up in the late 1800s and the early 1900s. The Texas Rangers was one of the earliest state agencies created originally as an effort to stop cattle rustlers. Often credited with being the first modern state agency was the Pennsylvania Constabulary (now known as the Pennsylvania State Police). It was formed to meet many needs of law enforcement, specifically at the state level.

Agencies at the state level are typically organized according to one of two models: centralized or decentralized. Centralized state law enforcement bodies are those that typically have one main organization or department under the umbrella of all state law enforcement.

Decentralized state law enforcement agencies often have several adjunct bodies that have their own powers and do not fall under one big umbrella. An example of this is the state law enforcement in North Carolina, which has several agencies with their own separate governing rules and organization. This includes (in North Carolina), a Highway Patrol and a State Bureau of Investigation, as well as smaller agencies like the Alcohol Beverage Control Board, and State Wildlife Commission.

LOCAL LAW ENFORCEMENT

Local law enforcement are those groups that we are accustomed to seeing on a regular basis. Whether the county Sheriff or the city police, these are agencies enforcing local laws and everyday violations.

Local city police organizations are modeled after early organizations in big cities like New York. Large agencies such as these are comprised of sworn officers as well as sometimes thousands of non-sworn staff, including administrative and support staff. City police are typically led by a Chief who is over the entire department. Chiefs are often appointed by the mayor and elected by the people or by the city council. Modern police agencies are organized by militaristic rank.

County law enforcement has waned. In many counties, although the Sheriff's department still exists, it often holds limited law enforcement duties and is regularly seen doing court duties such as acting as bailiffs and courthouse security.

*It is important to note that duties and roles are different throughout the country dependant on the city and state the agency is located in.

SOCIAL FUNCTION

Roles of the police may be slightly different depending on the law enforcement agency discussed. However, there are some basic social functions of police that are quite universal.

1. Enforce laws
2. Keep the peace
3. Prevent crimes
4. Protect rights
5. Provide services

The most obvious of these is enforcing laws. This is what we see the police doing on a daily basis when they pull people over for speeding or when they serve an arrest warrant.

Keeping the peace refers to maintaining a level of peace in the community. This can be seen when the police ticket a neighbor for having a loud party or when they perform crowd control at a local event. The role of keeping peace is important because oftentimes non-criminal peace violations can turn into criminal acts if left unchecked. How successful police are at keeping peace depends largely on the community's acceptance of this role. If the people of the community respect the officers and their suggestions to turn down the music (for example), then the peace will be maintained, largely due to the mutual respect.

Preventing crime is one of the main goals of patrol. Routine patrol can deter potential criminals from acting on urges that may be entertained if the police weren't around or active. Often in crime-laden neighborhoods you will see police presence increased simply to remind the people that the police are there and watching. This routine patrol along with working with juveniles, and educating the public, all prevent crime.
Police not only protect the rights of the law abiding citizens, but also the rights of the accused. This can be seen as one of the most important roles of policing. Responsible and effective policing occurs when the rights of the community are balanced with the due process rights of the accused.

We often call on police officers to provide services other than law enforcement. When we ask an officer for directions, have him intervene in an argument, or render emergency medical service, we are asking them to not act outside of their duties but to act as a service provider not just an enforcer of law.

POLICING STYLES

When it comes to policing there are as many different styles as there are individuals. Over time there have been terms applied to different types of behaviors, styles or strategies in policing. One policing philosophy is known as incident-driven policing. This type of policing is generally not considered to be particularly effective. The idea of incident-driven policing is to resolve specific instances of crimes. This attitude ignores recurring patterns and therefore rarely gets at the root of a problem. It can be frustrating and tedious.

Another type of policing philosophy which contrasts with incident-driven policing is problem-based policing. This strategy operates under theory that behind every incident of crime there is an underlying motive or problem. Problem-based policing requires attempting to identify and relieve this problem in order to stop future occurrences of the crime. It is important to understand that this philosophy attempts to find a universal cause for crime and strike at its society roots.

Situation-oriented policing is similar to problem-based policing in that it attempts to strike at the root of a problem, however it differs in that it believes that for each individual committing a crime there is a reason or motive that must be determined to stop it from occurring again. This style, therefore, looks for individual solutions rather than society as a whole. This style can also be referred to as a relative policing strategy.

In addition to these three crime philosophies there are three different styles of policing: watchman, legalistic, and service oriented. These styles often evolve from a public's perception of how an officer should act and what their responsibility is. The watchman style originates from a belief that the duty of the police officer is to maintain control and order in a society. As a result, certain crimes may be overlooked or underemphasized if they are minor or not important to maintaining order. This style tends to be less formal than the others, and centered around dispute resolution more than arrests and imprisonment – though enforcing the law is still an important element.

The legalistic style is nearly opposite of this mindset. This style places a large emphasis on the actual policing role of an officer, and a letter of the law approach to violations. Issuing citations and making arrests is considered very important, and the style tends to center around a more aggressive approach to and treatment of violators. The legalistic style also considers there to be one standard for all individuals, whereas the watchman style may recognize differences among individual situations.

Finally, the service style emphasizes the feeling that the officers responsibility is to protect individuals. Rather than enforcing the law being the most important factor, helping to improve the community and keeping everyone happy is considered the role of the officer. It tends to emphasize service roles of officers, such as traffic control.

ISSUES AND TRENDS FACING LAW ENFORCEMENT TODAY

PRIVATE POLICE

As with nearly every government organization, the private sector is creeping into policing. However, contrary to what you might think, private police agencies have been around for quite some time. Beginning with Allan Pinkerton's National Detective Agency in 1851, private detectives brought the private business into what was previously only a public entity. Early private security businesses, however, similar to pubic law enforcement of early times, had to deal with corruption. It was particularly bad in some early private agencies due to the lack of organization and proper training.

Now, private police agencies are credited with being able to adapt quickly and utilize new technology. This could be due, at least partly, to the fact that without public government, there is much less red tape and bureaucracy involved when something needs to be changed or added within the agency.

Some problems with private security, however, do exist. While some private agencies demand the utmost professionalism and truly strive to deliver quality results, some are simply not equipped to operate in the law enforcement sector. One critical difference between the private and public sector is accountability. Public sector law enforcement has to be accountable, not only to supervisors, but also to the public and more importantly to the ethics set forth for all government law enforcement bodies. There are strict guidelines and procedures that must be followed at every stage with the public law enforcement. However, in the private industry, the agencies are accountable only to themselves and their customers. If the customer allows a less than professional job, then the agency may not feel the need to step up their professionalism.

Private police agencies recognize this stigma and do their best to appear as professional and ethical law enforcement bodies. With specialized training and ongoing certifications, private security and policing has made great strides within the past several decades.

CORRUPTION

With great power comes great risk for corruption. Corruption in police agencies is not a new problem, mostly due to the power associated with the position and the lure of deviance. Police officers are tempted daily with minor deviances and more than likely have the opportunity for major criminal behavior as well.

Experts refer to two different types of police corruption. First is **occupational deviance**. Occupational deviance includes behavior that is motivated by personal gain. **Abuse of authority**, however, refers to acts that damage the goals of law enforcement, meaning the successful apprehension and conviction of criminals. For example, choosing not to ticket a friend for DUI after pulling them over would constitute an abuse of authority since it directly impedes the success of the criminal justice system.

Of course, corruption can be much larger than choosing not to give a citation to a friend. In 1971 Frank Serpico testified against friends and colleagues in front of the Knapp Commission in an effort to undo one of the largest and complex rings of corruption in New York City. Later made into a movie, Serpico's story is one of bravery in the face of corruption.

The Knapp Commission, established in 1970, found great corruption in New York City's Police Department and made several recommendations in an effort to reduce the problem. Those recommendations included holding commanders responsible for the actions of their subordinates, placing Internal Affairs offices within each precinct, and improving screening and recruiting practices for the Department. It was established then that police agencies needed greater accountability and controls were essential in making this happen.

Recognizing the problem, however, does not always create a solution. In the 1990s, William Hart, Police Chief of Detroit, was sentenced to serve up to ten years in federal prison for embezzling $2.6 million from a police fund. In 2006, the Henry County Virginia Sheriff's Department was broken up when a drug corruption scandal came to light. Officers were found to have been selling drugs and weapons from the department's evidence room, allowing evidence originally taken off the streets to be put right back where it came from. Eighteen people were arrested including the Sheriff himself. Corruption is an ongoing struggle that continues to plague law enforcement at all levels. In an effort to prevent such negative outcomes within organizations tasked with upholding the law, there are several steps that can be taken to prevent corruption.

1. Superior screening and recruiting practices. Most police agencies currently require psychological screening and testing to ensure that they are not knowingly bringing someone onto the force who may be predisposed to having problems.

2. Promoting accountability among the ranks. Holding superiors accountable for the actions of their subordinates requires more involvement on the part of the superiors with what is going on. The more they pay attention to what their officers are doing, the more likely they will be able to stop bad practices before they spin out of control.

3. Ask for the community's support. If the community understands that a free cup of coffee can lead to favors down the road, the responsible members will support the efforts of the department to stop these free practices.

4. Better training. Ongoing classes and ethics education can ensure there are no gray areas in what is considered acceptable and not acceptable.

With power comes a certain risk that corruption will occur. Controls in place today make it less common than 50 years ago, but it is a constant battle, nevertheless.

Occupational Characteristics

Many children play "cops and robbers" and many want to be police officers when they grow up. However, few actually become law enforcement. Pay could have a lot to do with this. Police officers are underpaid for the risks they face on a daily basis. And some of those who originally aspired to the position are just not qualified to deal with the daily stress and needs of the community.

There are several characteristics that agencies believe good police officers have.

- Reliability/Dependability: your fellow officers and the agency in general must be able to depend on you.

- Leadership: As a prominent community figure, you are expected to have the personality of a leader.

- Communication Skills: Officers must be able to talk to a variety of people and put them at ease when chaotic situations arise.

- Integrity: Officers are required to face ethical decisions on a daily basis and act according to the rules and ethics set forth for the department.

- Accuracy: When writing reports and dealing with evidence, accuracy is vital. The documents and records that officers keep may someday end up in a trial.

- Initiative: Not all actions taken by officers are orders passed down the chain; officers must be ready to act in a moment's notice and get things done when they need to be done.

- Humility: The role of police officer carries much power. A good officer can control her ego while remaining confident.

APPLICATION PROCESSES

Of course, how someone gets a job as a police officer depends on the agency they are trying to work for. But oftentimes police agencies follow loosely the same procedure when it comes to recruiting and hiring procedures.

1. Application

2. Informal Interview

3. Written and psychological examination

4. Physical test

5. Background investigation

6. Additional interviews

7. Medical examination

Typically college degrees are not required if one wishes to join a police force, but a college degree could raise the chances of being hired.

TRAINING

All police agencies send their new hires through some kind of initial training, usually consisting of classroom learning and on-the-job training. Some states mandate how many hours in a classroom setting must be completed both in the initial training stage as well as on an annual retraining basis. Oftentimes at these annual training classes, officers will be required to pass another physical assessment, ensuring that their fitness has not lagged in the past year.

POLICE CULTURE

The profession of law enforcement is unique and brings with it a culture unto itself. Officers work odd hours and deal with confidential situations they can't share with their civilian friends. They are also under high levels of stress and face public hostility. All of these circumstances lead to the culture of police. Often, police officers find themselves spending off duty hours with fellow officers and their families because they can identify with each other. The "blue code of silence" is a term used frequently to characterize the "we vs. them" mentality that often accompanies police work.

People who become officers often find that they lose their non-police friends and the stress of their job leads to stress in the home. High burnout and high levels of alcoholism are indicators that the stress involved with working as a police officer is very real.

Sample Test Questions

1) The term *mens rea* refers to:

   A) Guilty mind
   B) Guilty act
   C) The law of precedence
   D) Latin for "father of the people"

The correct answer is A:) Guilty mind.

2) When discussing elements of a crime, concurrence refers to:

   A) Presence of both harm and punishment
   B) Presence of both intent and the act
   C) Presence of actus reas and a harm
   D) The time causation of the crime

The correct answer is B:) Presence of both intent and the act. Concurrence of the act and intent designate a crime.

3) Which of the following terms describes a temporary delegation of parental rights by a parent to another individual?

   A) Mens rea
   B) Parenspatriae
   C) In loco parentis
   D) Actusreas

The correct answer is C:) In loco parentis. Some examples include a babysitter or schoolteacher.

4) Which term refers to laws written by legislative bodies with powers granted by the Constitution?

   A) Case law
   B) Procedural law
   C) Common law
   D) Statutory law

The correct answer is D:) Statutory law. Statutory law are those laws in the statutes.

5) What term means "to stand by what has been decided"?

    A) Parens patriae
    B) Stare decisis
    C) Actus reas
    D) Voir dire

The correct answer is B:) Stare decisis. Stare Decisis is the concept of precedence.

6) Which of the following most closely describes the case of Gideon v. Wainwright?

    A) Police entered and searched the defendant's home without a warrant. As a result, the evidence was deemed inadmissible in court under the Fourth Amendment.
    B) The Supreme Court ruled that the death sentence does not constitute cruel and unusual punishment, however that it did not apply to the defendant's case.
    C) Eight boys were sentenced to death after being rushed through a trial and receiving no chance to consult defense. The Supreme Court ruled that States must ensure due process.
    D) The Supreme Court ruled that jurisdictional waivers were valid in cases involving minors, as long as juvenile courts followed the correct procedures.

The correct answer is B:) The Supreme Court ruled that the death sentence does not constitute cruel and unusual punishment, however that it did not apply to the defendant's case.

7) When was the Magna Carta written?

    A) 1050
    B) 1215
    C) 1320
    D) 1510

The correct answer is B:) 1215. The Magna Carta was written in England in 1215 and constituted an agreement between the king and barons.

8) Criminology is defined as the scientific study of what?

    A) Criminal law and its applications
    B) Judicial powers
    C) Crime and applicable theories
    D) Police culture

The correct answer is C:) Crime and applicable theories.

9) Which of the following is NOT a characteristic of the Auburn System in prisons?

    A) Forced labor
    B) Perpetual solitary confinement
    C) Lockstep
    D) Silence

The correct answer is B:) Perpetual solitary confinement. Under the Auburn System, inmates would be in community settings during the day and in solitary confinement at night.

10) The idea of free will is central to which criminological theory?

    A) Positivist
    B) Classical
    C) Control
    D) Strain

The correct answer is B:) Classical. Classical theory attributes crime to a simple hedonistic principle.

11) Criminologist _____ developed positivist theory.

    A) Cesare Lombroso
    B) Cesare Beccaria
    C) Sigmeun Freud
    D) Cesare Basso

The correct answer is A:) Cesare Lombroso. Lombroso is considered the founder of positivist theory.

12) Police officers must obtain a search warrant to gather evidence due to which amendment?

    A) Fourth
    B) Sixth
    C) Eighth
    D) Fourteenth

The correct answer is A:) Fourth. The Fourth Amendment protects against unreasonable searches and seizures.

13) Which of the following is an example of victimless crime?

    A) Identity theft
    B) Drug possession
    C) Domestic violence
    D) Theft

The correct answer is B:) Drug possession. Drug possession is one of many crimes that some consider victimless.

14) Which of the following was created in 1929 by a group of police chiefs seeking a reliable way of compiling crime data?

    A) Universal Crime Report
    B) Uniform Crime Report
    C) Uniform Crime Regulations
    D) United States Crime Report

The correct answer is B:) Uniform Crime Report.

15) Also known as Part I offenses, these crimes are the major offenses cataloged in the UCR.

    A) Penal code
    B) Index crimes
    C) Felonies
    D) Clearance crimes

The correct answer is B:) Index crimes. The index crimes are the most serious offenses in the UCR.

16) Which of the following is NOT a status offense?

  A) Alcohol consumption
  B) Truancy and curfew violations
  C) Shoplifting
  D) Purchasing cigarettes

The correct answer is C:) Shoplifting. Shoplifting is illegal regardless of age or any other factor.

17) Which term refers to the amount of reported crimes that have ended in arrest?

  A) Index rate
  B) Crime rate
  C) Arrest rate
  D) Clearance rate

The correct answer is D:) Clearance rate. This rate is often used in conjunction with the crime rate in analyzing data.

18) Which amendment was invoked in the case of Atkins v. Virginia?

  A) Fifth
  B) Eighth
  C) Tenth
  D) Twelfth

The correct answer is B:) Eighth. The case of Atkins v. Virginia resulted in the Supreme Court ruling that it is against the Eighth Amendment for mentally retarded individuals to be given the death penalty.

19) This agency is tasked with compiling and publishing data collected in the UCR:

  A) Bureau of Justice Statistics
  B) Federal Bureau of Investigation
  C) Local law enforcement agencies
  D) Central Intelligence Agency

The correct answer is B:) Federal Bureau of Investigation. The FBI is the clearinghouse for the data in the UCR.

20) The following crime is not included in the UCR:

   A) Possession of illegal substances
   B) Drug trafficking
   C) Federal offenses
   D) All of the above

The correct answer is D:) All of the above. No drug offenses or federal crimes are indexed in the UCR.

21) What was the most important issue questioned in the case of Powell v. Alabama?

   A) Right to a lawyer
   B) Right to a speedy trial
   C) Right to call witnesses
   D) Right to consult peers

The correct answer is A:) Right to a lawyer. The Supreme Court ruled that "a defendant, charged with a serious crime, must not be stripped of his right to have sufficient time to advise with counsel and prepare his defense."

22) Which of the following is a self reporting survey used to measure crime?

   A) NCVS
   B) UCR
   C) NIBRS
   D) All of the above

The correct answer is A:) NCVS. The National Crime Victimization Survey is a self reporting survey.

23) Which of the following is NOT a protection of the Sixth Amendment?

   A) Right to a speedy and public trial
   B) The accused must know what they are accused of
   C) The accused must be allowed to have witnesses in their favor
   D) Protection against being tried twice for the same crime

The correct answer is D:) Protection against being tried twice for the same crime. This is a protection extended by the Fifth Amendment.

24) In the case of Hudson v. Palmer, which Constitutional Amendment was invoked?

    A) First
    B) Fourth
    C) Seventh
    D) Eighth

The correct answer is B:) Fourth.

25) Which of the following best describes the case of Kent v. United States?

    A) Police entered and searched the defendant's home without a warrant. As a result, the evidence was deemed inadmissible in court under the Fourth Amendment.
    B) A prison inmate argued that he was unfairly treated in a locker search. As a result, the Supreme Court ruled that the Fourth Amendment does not apply to inmates.
    C) Eight boys were sentenced to death after being rushed through a trial and receiving no chance to consult defense. The Supreme Court ruled that States must ensure due process.
    D) The Supreme Court ruled that jurisdictional waivers were valid in cases involving minors, as long as juvenile courts followed the correct procedures.

The correct answer is D:) The Supreme Court ruled that jurisdictional waivers were valid in cases involving minors, as long as juvenile courts followed the correct procedures.

26) In the Middle Ages, at which age did a child become an adult?

    A) 7
    B) 14
    C) 16
    D) 12

The correct answer is B:) 14. Fourteen was considered the age at which a child could begin to take responsibility for their actions.

27) In the case of Mapp v. Ohio, which Constitutional Amendment was invoked?

A) First
B) Fourth
C) Seventh
D) Eighth

The correct answer is B:) Fourth. The Supreme Court ruled that evidence obtained in violation of the Fourth Amendment may not be used in criminal cases.

28) What is the term used to refer to juveniles who did not receive proper care from their parents?

A) Delinquent
B) Dependant
C) Undisciplined
D) Neglected

The correct answer is D:) Neglected. Neglected children have not been cared for properly.

29) What is testimony?

A) Verbal statements given under oath
B) Written documents
C) Oral history of an event
D) None of the above

The correct answer is A:) Verbal statements given under oath. These statements are used in trial.

30) The creation of a Juvenile Court System came:

A) In 1935 with the creation of houses of refuge.
B) In 1898 and the passing of the Children's Welfare Act.
C) In 1938 and the passing of the Juvenile Court Act.
D) After the abolition of state sponsored whippings.

The correct answer is C:) In 1938 and the passing of the Juvenile Court Act. This act was the first that established a separate court for juvenile cases.

31) Which criminological theory looks at what prevents people from committing crime, rather than what causes people to commit crime?

    A) Control theory
    B) Labeling theory
    C) Classical theory
    D) Strain theory

The correct answer is A:) Control theory. Control theory, unlike other criminological theories tries to explain what stops people from committing crimes.

32) Why do we classify or categorize crimes?

    A) To assist in organizing and compiling data
    B) To analyze causation
    C) To predict future trends
    D) All of the above

The correct answer is D:) All of the above. Categorizing crimes allows us to organize and compile data as well as analyze causation and predict future trends.

33) The decision in which case disallows the death penalty for mentally retarded individuals?

    A) Hudson v. Palmer
    B) Gregg v. Georgia
    C) Mapp v. Ohio
    D) Atkins v. Virginia

The correct answer is D:) Atkins v. Virginia. The case of Atkins v. Virginia resulted in the Supreme Court ruling that it is against the Eighth Amendment for mentally retarded individuals to be given the death penalty.

34) Which of the following refers to crimes that go unreported to police and otherwise undetected?

    A) Thin blue line
    B) Crime shadow
    C) Dark figure of crime
    D) Clearance rate

The correct answer is C:) Dark figure of crime. Measuring the dark figure of crime is a constant struggle for law enforcement.

35) One of the first theories used to explain the phenomenon of youth crime was:

   A) Labeling theory
   B) Conflict theory
   C) The theory of social disinterest
   D) Social ecology theory

The correct answer is D:) Social ecology theory. Social ecology theory explains delinquency by attributing it to social disorganization.

36) A minor who commits a crime is a

   A) Juvenile delinquent
   B) Misunderstood minor
   C) Status offender
   D) None of the above

The correct answer is A:) Juvenile delinquent. Juvenile delinquency can occur in the form of virtually any type of crime, ranging from more serious violent crimes, to simple status offenses.

37) Which was the first U.S. Supreme Court case that recognized the need for due process rights for juveniles?

   A) In Re Gault
   B) Kent v. U.S.
   C) Gideon v. Wainwright
   D) Mapp v. Ohio

The correct answer is B:) Kent v. U.S. This case recognized that juveniles were entitled to due process rights particularly when transferring a case to adult court.

38) What body of early law originated in ancient Babylon?

   A) The twelve tablets
   B) Code of Hammurabi
   C) Magna Carta
   D) Justinian Code

The answer is B:) Code of Hammurabi. This code is one of the earliest examples of written law.

39) Status offenses are generally committed by

  A) Minors
  B) Mentally ill people
  C) Adults
  D) Business owners

The correct answer is A:) Minors. For example, drinking alcohol, truancy, possession of a firearm and purchasing cigarettes are all exclusively juvenile crimes.

40) This early body of law separated law, for the first time, into private and public law:

  A) Justinian Code
  B) Twelve Tablets
  C) Feudal Law
  D) English Common Law

The correct answer is A:) Justinian Code. The Justinian Code contained elements of what we know today as our civil and criminal laws.

41) Which of the following was made up of English customs, rules, and judicial rulings?

  A) Case law
  B) Magna Carta
  C) Feudal law
  D) Common law

The correct answer is D:) Common law. Common law was the basis for the original traditional laws in the United States.

42) Which term refers to laws that are on the books but not necessarily immoral?

  A) Mala in se
  B) Mala prohibita
  C) Mens rea
  D) Lex talions

The correct answer is B:) Mala prohibita. Mala prohibita are laws that maybe prohibited but would not be considered immoral were they not written laws.

43) Which of the following BEST describes lockstep?

  A) Prisoners are chained to a rail attached at the base of a wall, ensuring that they go only where they are permitted.
  B) Prisoners feet are all chained together, forcing them to step in sync and stopping them from rioting.
  C) Prisoners travel in a close, single file line with one hand on the person in front of them and stepping in sync.
  D) None of the above

The correct answer is C:) Prisoners travel in a close, single file line with one hand on the person in front of them and stepping in sync. Lockstep is an important practice of the Auburn Prison System.

44) Which of the following Amendments in the Bill of Rights concerns the concept of due process?

  A) 4th
  B) 5th
  C) 14th
  D) All the above

The correct answer is D:) All the above. The 4th, 5th, and 14th Amendments encompass the issues related to due process.

45) Which of the following had an extreme impact on the courts in regards to due process?

  A) The Warren Court
  B) UCR
  C) Juvenile Justice Act
  D) Frankpledge system

The correct answer is A:) The Warren Court. Under Chief Justice Earl Warren, the Supreme Court ruled in favor of the rights of the accused and protecting individual rights.

46) The purpose of the NCVS program is to

A) Rank various agencies within the United States government.
B) Produce reliable and useful statistical information.
C) Identify areas with ineffective crime fighting strategies.
D) Determine the number of people who are the victims of crimes.

The correct answer is D:) Determine the number of people who are the victims of crimes. Its survey format is thought to be more reliable than the UCR's crime report base.

47) This model of justice focuses on protecting individual's rights in the court system:

A) Crime control model
B) Due process model
C) Retributive model
D) Model of mala in se

The correct answer is B:) Due process model. The due process model of justice's main focus is the protection of individual rights.

48) What is a lictor?

A) An Egyptian soldier tasked with protecting the pharaoh
B) An early Greek police officer who acted as judge, jury, and executioner
C) A Roman firefighter who also shared law enforcement duties
D) A Roman guard to the magistrate

The correct answer is D:) A Roman guard to the magistrate. Lictors were responsible for bringing the accused before the magistrate and guarding the magistrate.

49) A judge would not set bail at 20 million dollars for a person accused of stealing a corn dog because of which amendment?

A) Fourth
B) Sixth
C) Eighth
D) Fourteenth

The correct answer is C:) Eighth. The Eighth Amendment protects against excessive bail and cruel and unusual punishments.

50) What was the tithing system?

   A) A self governing system in place to prevent the need for public law enforcement
   B) A hierarchal system of lords and vassals
   C) A religious system focused on paying dues to the Church
   D) None of the above

The correct answer is A:) A self governing system in place to prevent the need for public law enforcement. The tithing system put citizen's responsible for each other.

51) Approximately what percent of female inmates are affected by pregnancy?

   A) 10%
   B) 20%
   C) 40%
   D) 60%

The correct answer is A:) 10%. Certain health care issues such as pregnancy affect an estimated 7-10 percent of female inmates, with the trend rising over time.

52) This early London Police force was developed by Magistrate Henry Fielding:

   A) Bell Street Runners
   B) Bobbies
   C) Bow Street Runners
   D) None of the above

The correct answer is C:) Bow Street Runners. The Bow Street Runners were named after the Street that Magistrate Fielding worked off of.

53) Which of the following was NOT a result of the Kansas City Patrol experiment?

   A) Valuable information about the effects of police work was gathered.
   B) It was demonstrated that safe and effective experiments could be carried out relative to police work.
   C) Police were able to determine that visible police presence does reduce the levels of crime.
   D) All of the above are results of the Kansas City Patrol experiment.

The correct answer is C:) Police were able to determine that visible police presence does reduce the levels of crime. In fact, the study had the opposite results.

54) In what year did Sir Robert Peel begin developing the famous London Metropolitan Police Department?

    A) 1928
    B) 1829
    C) 1846
    D) 1903

The correct answer is B:) 1829. In 1829, Sir Peel created the historic London Metropolitan Police force.

55) What activity did the London Metropolitan Police know could significantly deter crime?

    A) Harsh sentences from the court
    B) Curfews
    C) Patrol
    D) High arrest rates

The correct answer is C:) Patrol. The police force knew that significant patrol would reduce crime by deterrence.

56) Which case established the power of judicial review?

    A) Hudson v. Palmer
    B) Terry v. Ohio
    C) Powell v. Alabama
    D) Marbury v. Madison

The correct answer is D:) Marbury v. Madison. The Supreme Court ruled that he did have a right to the position. However, they also ruled that the Constitution did not give the court the right to force the point, and stated that it was their right to determine whether or not certain acts of Congress or the President were Constitutional.

57) The original FBI was merely a department under the umbrella of which agency?

    A) Bureau of Internal Revenue
    B) Department of Justice
    C) Crime Commission
    D) Bureau of Justice Statistics

The correct answer is B:) Department of Justice. Prior to becoming a force onto itself, the FBI acted under the DOJ.

58) The Drug Enforcement Agency (DEA) as we know it today was given its name under which piece of legislation?

    A) Harrison Narcotics Act
    B) Comprehensive Drug Abuse Prevention and Control Act
    C) Crime Control Act
    D) Illegal Substance Control Act

The correct answer is B:) Comprehensive Drug Abuse Prevention and Control Act. This act named and assigned duties to the DEA.

59) Which of the following most closely describes the case of Terry v. Ohio?

    A) The defendant argued that a police officer searching his person constituted unreasonable search and seizure, and all evidence should be inadmissible. The Supreme Court ruled otherwise.
    B) A prison inmate argued that he was unfairly treated in a locker search. As a result, the Supreme Court ruled that the Fourth Amendment does not apply to inmates.
    C) The defendant argued that he had a right to an appointment made by a previous president, and the Supreme Court agreed and established the power of judicial review.
    D) Police entered and searched the defendant's home without a warrant. As a result, the evidence was deemed inadmissible in court under the Fourth Amendment.

The correct answer is A:) The defendant argued that a police officer searching his person constituted unreasonable search and seizure, and all evidence should be inadmissible. The Supreme Court ruled otherwise.

60) The ability of police to keep the peace depends largely on:

    A) Community's respect
    B) Powers granted to the police
    C) Due process
    D) Neighborhood dynamics

The correct answer is A:) Community's respect. If the community does not respect the police, what reason is there for them to comply with an officer's wishes.

61) Which of the following terms describes the right of the government to intervene when parents are not meeting the health and safety needs of their children?

A) Mens rea
B) Parenspatriae
C) In loco parentis
D) Actusreas

The correct answer is B:) Parenspatriae. The theory is that the government is the ultimate "parent" or protector of all individuals and it is their right and duty to step in when parents are irresponsible.

62) What is original jurisdiction?

A) Authority given to a court to be the first court to hear the matter
B) Courts must hear the cases brought to them
C) The Supreme Court's right to evaluate and review any decisions and actions by any Court or governmental agency in the country
D) None of the above

The correct answer is A:) Authority given to a court to be the first court to hear the matter. Original jurisdiction allows the court to hear the original case.

63) Who confirms Presidential nominations to federal district court judgeships?

A) Congress
B) Members of the Presidential political party who serve in the House
C) Senate Judiciary Committee
D) Senate Nominations Board

The correct answer is C:) Senate Judiciary Committee. The Senate Judiciary Committee confirms all federal court nominations.

64) Which amendment protects a person from self-incrimination?

A) Fourth
B) Third
C) Fifth
D) Fourteenth

The correct answer is C:) Fifth. The Fifth Amendment additionally protects against double jeopardy, and ensures due process.

65) Which of the following most closely describes the case of Gideon v. Wainwright?
   A) Police entered and searched the defendant's home without a warrant. As a result, the evidence was deemed inadmissible in court under the Fourth Amendment.
   B) A prison inmate argued that he was unfairly treated in a locker search. As a result, the Supreme Court ruled that the Fourth Amendment does not apply to inmates.
   C) The defendant could not afford a lawyer and the Supreme Court ruled that under the Fourteenth Amendment the court must appoint a lawyer in all criminal cases in which this is the case.
   D) Eight boys were sentenced to death after being rushed through a trial and receiving no chance to consult defense. The Supreme Court ruled that States must ensure due process.

The correct answer is C:) The defendant could not afford a lawyer and the Supreme Court ruled that under the Fourteenth Amendment the court must appoint a lawyer in all criminal cases in which this is the case.

66) What are the two types of police corruption?

   A) Occupational deviance and abuse of authority
   B) Moral disobedience and abuse of authority
   C) Legal and moral
   D) Ethical deficiency and labor deviance

The correct answer is A:) Occupational deviance and abuse of authority. These can be defined as corruption for personal gain or at the expense of the purpose of law enforcement.

67) Which of the following BEST describes retribution?

   A) Imprisonment is the just punishment for committing a crime.
   B) Criminals should be forced to compensate victims for any damage they inflicted.
   C) Imprisonment allows an opportunity for criminals to be reeducated and introduced into society.
   D) None of the above

The correct answer is A:) Imprisonment is the just punishment for committing a crime. It is basically the idea that the criminal deserves to be jailed for breaking the law, in and of itself.

68) Which of the following was suggested by the Knapp Commission of 1970?

    A) Improving screening and recruiting practices
    B) Holding commanders responsible for the actions of their subordinates
    C) Placing Internal Affairs offices within each precinct
    D) All of the above

The correct answer is D:) All of the above. The Knapp commission made several recommendations to help reduce corruption in law enforcement.

69) How many Federal District Courts are there in the United States federal system?

    A) 95
    B) 97
    C) 94
    D) 83

The correct answer is C:) 94. There are 94 courts in the United States and Puerto Rico, Guam, Virgin Islands and the Northern Mariana Islands.

70) The UCR Program is an effort to

    A) Rank various agencies within the United States government.
    B) Produce reliable and useful statistical information.
    C) Identify areas with ineffective crime fighting strategies.
    D) Determine the number of people who are the victims of crimes.

The correct answer is B:) Produce reliable and useful statistical information. The UCR Program can give valuable information about crime levels and distributions, but should not be used as a ranking system.

71) Which body of rules dictates how the U.S. Courts of Appeals should handle their proceedings?

    A) Appellate Laws of Procedure
    B) Federal Rules of Appellate Procedure
    C) Rules of Engagement
    D) 15th Amendment

The correct answer is B:) Federal Rules of Appellate Procedure.

72) The Supreme Court's greatest power lies in

   A) Appellate jurisdiction
   B) Constitutional review
   C) Judicial review
   D) None of the above

The correct answer is C:) Judicial review. Judicial review allows the court to evaluate and review any decisions and actions by any court or governmental agency in the Country.

73) The Federal Air Marshal Service operates under which department?

   A) Department of Homeland Security
   B) Department of Airline Operations
   C) Department of Justice
   D) Department of Civil Protection

The correct answer is A:) Department of Homeland Security.

74) Approximately what is the ratio of inmates to correctional officers in federal prisons?

   A) 3
   B) 5
   C) 10
   D) 20

The correct answer is C:) 10. More precisely, in 2005 it was measured to be 10.3.

75) Which Supreme Court case established the Court as the final Constitutional interpreter?

   A) In Re Gault
   B) Mapp v. Ohio
   C) Griffin v. California
   D) Marbury v. Madison

The correct answer is D:) Marbury v. Madison. This case, under Chief Justice John Marshall, cemented the powers of the Supreme Court.

76) Which of the following policing philosophies believes that it is most important to resolve and stop individual incidents of crime?

   A) Authoritarian-minded
   B) Incident-driven
   C) Problem based
   D) Situation oriented

The correct answer is B:) Incident-driven. This attitude ignores recurring patterns and therefore rarely gets at the root of a problem.

77) What is constitutes a "term" of the Supreme Court?

   A) 8 months, from February to September
   B) 10 months, from February to November
   C) 10 months, from September to June
   D) 10 months, from October to July

The correct answer is D:) 10 months, from October to July. The Supreme Court sits for one of these ten month terms per year.

78) Which of the following is NOT a responsibility of the FDA?

   A) Ensuring the safety and sanitation of products which come into contact with people
   B) Mandating which drugs are illegal
   C) Regulating the safety of food products
   D) Preventing the use of illegal drugs

The correct answer is D:) Preventing the use of illegal drugs. This is the responsibility of the DEA.

79) In which state, through a referee system of justice, did the term "justice of the peace" come from?

   A) New Jersey
   B) California
   C) Massachusetts
   D) Pennsylvania

The correct answer is D:) Pennsylvania. An early system of referees had a "peace-maker" rule on conflicts. This is where the term "justice of the peace" came from.

80) The Miranda Rights are read to ensure that a suspect understands the rights afforded by which Constitutional Amendment?

A) First
B) Fourth
C) Fifth
D) Sixth

The correct answer is C:) Fifth. Specifically, the Miranda Rights are meant to protect a suspect against inadvertent self-incrimination.

81) Courts of limited jurisdiction are which of the following?

A) Courts that have the right to hear a matter for the first time
B) Lower courts that handle minor criminal issues
C) Higher state courts that hear only felonies
D) None of the above

The correct answer is B:) Lower courts that handle minor criminal issues. These are state courts directly underneath courts of general jurisdiction.

82) Approximately how many incarcerated women have children under the age of 18?

A) 10%
B) 20%
C) 40%
D) 60%

The correct answer is D:) 60%. Around two thirds of incarcerated women have children under the age of 18 – having anywhere from one to more than five children.

83) Which of the following is a true statement?

A) States usually have one type of appeals court
B) States always have an intermediate appeals court
C) Some states do not have a state Supreme Court
D) None of the above

The correct answer is D:) None of the above. Most states have more than one type of appeals court; all states have a supreme court, and not all states have an intermediate appeals court.

84) Which of the following most closely describes the case of Mapp v. Ohio?

A) Police entered and searched the defendant's home without a warrant. As a result, the evidence was deemed inadmissible in court under the Fourth Amendment.
B) A prison inmate argued that he was unfairly treated in a locker search. As a result, the Supreme Court ruled that the Fourth Amendment does not apply to inmates.
C) The defendant could not afford a lawyer and the Supreme Court ruled that under the Fourteenth Amendment the court must appoint a lawyer in all criminal cases in which this is the case.
D) Eight boys were sentenced to death after being rushed through a trial and receiving no chance to consult defense. The Supreme Court ruled that States must ensure due process.

The correct answer is A:) Police entered and searched the defendant's home without a warrant. As a result, the evidence was deemed inadmissible in court under the Fourth Amendment.

85) What is the standard of proof in U.S. adult criminal court cases?

A) Beyond a reasonable doubt
B) Beyond the shadow of a doubt
C) Without doubt
D) Innocent until proven guilty

The correct answer is A:) Beyond a reasonable doubt. The prosecution must prove, beyond a reasonable doubt, that the defendant committed the crime.

86) The purpose of the Federal Air Marshal Service is to

A) Ensure that all flights in the United States have detailed schedules that don't conflict.
B) Ensure the safety and security of individuals in the United States traveling by plane.
C) Thoroughly examine all individuals employed by airlines to ensure their competence.
D) Set regulations governing airline procedures.

The correct answer is B:) Ensure the safety and security of individuals in the United States traveling by plane. It is the job of Federal Air Marshals to blend in with other individuals on flights and watch for potential problems.

87) Community incarceration is

   A) Parole
   B) Allocution
   C) Shock sentence
   D) Probation

The correct answer is D:) Probation. Community incarceration is a type of probationary status in which the defendant is not sent to jail, but they are monitored and must follow a set of instructions.

88) What was the first document to refer to due process?

   A) Magna Carta
   B) Declaration of Independence
   C) Bill of Rights
   D) Constitution

The correct answer is A:) Magna Carta. This is one of the two important elements of the Magna Carta which influenced the U.S. Constitution.

89) An arraignment is

   A) Held to determine if probable cause exists to bind the case over to trial
   B) Held to establish the burden of proof
   C) The first appearance in court
   D) Usually a lengthy formal process

The correct answer is C:) The first appearance in court. The arraignment is used to inform the offender of their charges and give them an opportunity to make a plea.

90) A preliminary hearing is:

   A) Held to establish the burden of proof
   B) The first appearance in court
   C) Held to determine if probable cause exists to bind the case over to trial
   D) None of the above

The correct answer is C:) Held to determine if probable cause exists to bind the case over to trial. The preliminary hearing resembles a trial but is not to determine guilt or innocence.

91) Which of the following Constitutional Amendments was invoked in the case of Terry v. Ohio?

A) First
B) Third
C) Fourth
D) Eighth

The correct answer is C:) Fourth. Terry argued that the random searched constituted an unreasonable search and seizure and therefore it was a violation of the Fourth Amendment and the evidence found during it should not be allowed in court.

92) Which of the following are challenges for an attorney to raise to dismiss potential jurors?

A) Challenges to the array
B) Preliminary challenges
C) Challenges to the venue
D) All of the above

The correct answer is A:) Challenges to the array. These are used when one side believes that the jury pool is either not reflective of the community or that the pool is biased.

93) When a judge sentences an individual to a certain amount of time in jail followed by a certain amount of time on parole, it is referred to as

A) Allocution
B) Community incarceration
C) Shock probation
D) Split sentence

The correct answer is D:) Split sentence. The sentence is split between jail and probation. This is not to be confused with shock probation.

94) Where did common law originate?

A) 17th century France
B) 15th century England
C) 14th century France
D) 13th century England

The correct answer is D:) 13th century England.

95) What might be the purpose of allocution?

   A) It is a chance for a defendant to make a last minute personal appeal to a jury or judge.
   B) It is a chance for an officer to admit that they were involved in illegal seizure of evidence.
   C) It is a technicality on which a defendant in a criminal case may make an appeal.
   D) It refers to a situation in which a parent temporarily delegates responsibility for their children.

The correct answer is A:) It is a chance for a defendant to make a last minute personal appeal to a jury or judge. The term allocution refers to when, during or just prior to sentencing, a judge gives the defendant a chance to speak on their own behalf.

96) The following term refers to the removal of a juror without having to show cause:

   A) Perfunctory challenge
   B) Peremptory challenge
   C) Presumptive challenge
   D) None of the above

The correct answer is B:) Peremptory challenge. Attorneys do not have to show cause for dismissal when using a peremptory challenge.

97) Which policing style places an emphasis on the role of an officer in protecting and improving the community?

   A) Service
   B) Legalistic
   C) Watchman
   D) Improvement minded

The correct answer is A:) Service. Rather than enforcing the law being the most important factor, helping to improve the community and keep everyone happy is considered the role of the officer. It tends to emphasize service roles of officers, such as traffic control.

98) Which of the following is true about circumstantial evidence?

    A) It is inadmissible in court
    B) It represents the majority of evidence submitted at trial
    C) Both A & B
    D) None of the above

The correct answer is B:) It represents the majority of evidence submitted at trial. Circumstantial evidence requires interpretation.

99) What was significant about the Supreme Court case, Griffin v. California?

    A) It allowed for the admission of circumstantial evidence
    B) It protected the rules of evidence
    C) It stated that invoking the 5th Amendment could not be considered an admission of guilt
    D) It was found in violation of the 5th Amendment

The correct answer is C:) It stated that invoking the 5th Amendment could not be considered an admission of guilt.

100) When an individual is sent to prison for a few months and then the rest of the sentence is waived and they are let out on probation it is referred to as

    A) Allocution
    B) Community incarceration
    C) Shock probation
    D) Split sentence

The correct answer is C:) Shock probation. The idea behind shock probation is that for some criminals, a short time in jail is enough to "shock" them out of a criminal lifestyle.

101) Which of the following policing philosophies believes that all individuals have their own reasons for committing crimes which must be considered?

    A) Authoritarian-minded
    B) Incident-driven
    C) Problem based
    D) Situation oriented

The correct answer is D:) Situation oriented. The problem based method is the opinion that crime in general has an underlying cause which must be discovered.

102) Which of the following is true about hearsay?

    A) It is nearly always inadmissible in court
    B) It involves improper application of the 5th Amendment
    C) It represents the largest portion of evidence submitted at trial
    D) None of the above

The correct answer is A:) It is nearly inadmissible in court. Hearsay is inadmissible except in rare cases.

103) How many times can a witness be examined and cross-examined?

    A) Four times per side
    B) Only once
    C) Until the judge is satisfied
    D) Until both sides are satisfied

The correct answer is D:) Until both sides are satisfied. This process of examination and cross-examination can go on indefinitely.

104) Which of the following agencies determines which drugs are illegal?

    A) FDA
    B) DEA
    C) DOD
    D) FBI

The correct answer is A:) FDA. The DEA, on the other hand, works to prevent people from abusing drugs and to regulate their use.

105) What can happen when a jury is deadlocked?

    A) A mistrial
    B) The judge "recharges" them
    C) One person will not change their mind
    D) All of the above

The correct answer is D:) All of the above. A deadlocked jury is often caused by one person not willing to change their mind, this is dealt with by mistrial or the judge recharging the jury.

106) Which of the following statements is TRUE?

A) The inmate to correctional officer ratio is decreasing at both state and federal levels.
B) The inmate to correctional officer ratio is increasing at state and decreasing at federal levels.
C) The inmate to correctional officer ratio is decreasing at state and increasing at federal levels.
D) The inmate to correctional officer ratio is increasing at both state and federal levels.

The correct answer is D:) The inmate to correctional officer ratio is increasing at both state and federal levels. This is true despite the fact that the number of facilities is also increasing with time.

107) A legal system which has a set of universal laws, interpreted in specific cases by judges is characteristic of

A) Civil law
B) Universal law
C) Common law
D) Natural law

The correct answer is C:) Common law. Common law systems contrast with civil law systems which extensively classify every type of crime and its associated punishment, not allowing room for interpretation.

108) Who typically does the pre-sentence investigation?

A) The judge
B) Police officer
C) Probation officer
D) Health and Human Services worker

The correct answer is C:) Probation officer. A probation officer typically prepares the pre-sentence report and makes a sentencing recommendation to the court.

109) Which of the following most closely describes the case of Hudson v. Palmer?

    A) Police entered and searched the defendant's home without a warrant. As a result, the evidence was deemed inadmissible in court under the Fourth Amendment.

    B) A prison inmate argued that he was unfairly treated in a locker search. As a result, the Supreme Court ruled that the Fourth Amendment does not apply to inmates.

    C) The defendant could not afford a lawyer and the Supreme Court ruled that under the Fourteenth Amendment the court must appoint a lawyer in all criminal cases in which this is the case.

    D) Eight boys were sentenced to death after being rushed through a trial and receiving no chance to consult defense. The Supreme Court ruled that States must ensure due process.

The correct answer is B:) A prison inmate argued that he was unfairly treated in a locker search. As a result, the Supreme Court ruled that the Fourth Amendment does not apply to inmates.

110) Which of the following most closely describes the case of Powell v. Alabama?

    A) Police entered and searched the defendant's home without a warrant. As a result, the evidence was deemed inadmissible in court under the Fourth Amendment.

    B) A prison inmate argued that he was unfairly treated in a locker search. As a result, the Supreme Court ruled that the Fourth Amendment does not apply to inmates.

    C) The defendant could not afford a lawyer and the Supreme Court ruled that under the Fourteenth Amendment the court must appoint a lawyer in all criminal cases in which this is the case.

    D) Eight boys were sentenced to death after being rushed through a trial and receiving no chance to consult defense. The Supreme Court ruled that States must ensure due process.

The correct answer is D:) Eight boys were sentenced to death after being rushed through a trial and receiving no chance to consult defense. The Supreme Court ruled that States must ensure due process.

111) Which of the following is true about indeterminate sentencing?

    A) It encourages rehabilitation
    B) It allows for significant judicial discretion
    C) It may be to blame for sentencing disparities
    D) All of the above

The correct answer is D:) All of the above. Indeterminate sentencing allows judges to used their discretion in choosing a sentence right for the individual. This may cause judicial abuse and sentencing disparities. It also encourages rehabilitation.

112) Which of the following is true about Federal Sentencing Guidelines?

    A) They are mandatory
    B) They are optional
    C) They are an example of determinate sentencing
    D) B & C

The correct answer is D:) B & C. These guidelines were made optional in 2005 and represent determinate sentencing.

113) Which of the following is a document taken out in juvenile court alleging the child is delinquent or in other ways in need of court intervention?

    A) Citation
    B) Juvenile summons
    C) Juvenile petition
    D) Complaint

The correct answer is C:) Juvenile petition. Juvenile petitions are similar to a criminal complaint in adult courts.

114) When are detention hearings held in juvenile courts?

    A) Within 24 hours of apprehension
    B) Within 24 hours of the preliminary hearing
    C) Within 72 hours of apprehension
    D) None of the above

The correct answer is A:) Within 24 hours of apprehension. The juvenile system does not want to detain juvenile offenders any longer than absolutely necessary.

115) The trial of a juvenile is referred to as:

    A) Adjudication hearing
    B) Delinquency hearing
    C) Disposition hearing
    D) None of the above

The correct answer is A:) Adjudication hearing. The adjudication hearing has many similarities to an adult court but is much more informal and laid back in nature.

116) The commonly recognized goals of sentencing are:

    A) Deterrence, rehabilitation, incapacitation, and adjudication
    B) Deterrence, restitution, incapacitation, and rehabilitation
    C) Deterrence, rehabilitation, incapacitation, and retribution
    D) Divergence, retribution, rehabilitation, and incapacitation

The correct answer is C:) Deterrence, rehabilitation, incapacitation, and retribution. These make up the goals of sentencing.

117) When a judge gives a defendant the opportunity to speak before sentencing, it is called

    A) Mens rea
    B) Shock probation
    C) Allocution
    D) Magna carta

The correct answer is C:) Allocution. During allocution the defendant is not sworn in and what they say is not subject to cross examination.

118) Which of the following is when a sentence serves as an example to deter others from committing the same type of crime?

    A) Specific deterrence
    B) General deterrence
    C) Divergence
    D) None of the above

The correct answer is B:) General deterrence.

119) Which of the following Constitutional Amendments was invoked in the case of Gregg v. Georgia?

A) Fourth
B) Eighth
C) Tenth
D) Fourteenth

The correct answer is B:) Eighth. The court ruled that the death penalty did not constitute cruel and unusual punishment.

120) Which is the earliest know goal of sentencing?

A) Retribution
B) Annihilation
C) Deterrence
D) Incapacitation

The correct answer is A:) Retribution. Revenge was the earliest goal of sentencing and punishment.

121) Which of the following BEST describes the broken window theory?

A) If an area has a lot of broken windows it is likely that little crime actually occurs in the area.
B) The best way to test whether an individual has delinquent tendencies is to walk them past a broken window and see their reaction.
C) Ill-kept neighborhoods encourage crime by speaking to a lower standard of law adherence and care.
D) The best way to prevent theft is by having broken windows because they indicate that there is nothing of value to steal.

The correct answer is C:) Ill-kept neighborhoods encourage crime by speaking to a lower standard of law adherence and care. The theory was originally proposed by scientists James Wilson and George Kelling.

122) The validity of which of the following was called into question in the case of Kent v. U.S.?

A) Second Amendment
B) Magna Carta
C) Jurisdictional waiver
D) Shock probation

The correct answer is C:) Jurisdictional waiver. Because he was under 18, Kent was under the jurisdiction of the juvenile court unless they were to sign a jurisdictional waiver after investigating it themselves, which they did. However, Kent appealed on the basis that the waiver was invalid.

123) Which of the following is an example of incapacitation?

A) Imprisonment
B) Capital punishment
C) Chemical castration
D) All of the above

The correct answer is D:) All of the above. Incapacitation seeks to remove the offender's ability to commit future crimes.

124) The Auburn system of prisons featured

A) Hard work done in silence
B) Solitary confinement with only a Bible to read
C) Dormitory housing
D) None of the above

The correct answer is A:) Hard work done in silence. The Auburn system was compared to slavery by critics.

125) Prisons that capitalized on the free labor of inmates were called:

A) Industrial prisons
B) Labor camps
C) Mechanical prisons
D) All of the above

The correct answer is A:) Industrial prisons. Coming about in the industrial age, these prisons made a profit off of the free labor at their fingertips.

126) From the 1940s through the 1960s American prisons went through a period advocating treatment. What was this referred to as?

A) Medical model
B) Psychology model
C) Treatment era
D) Rehabilitative model

The correct answer is A:) Medical model. The medical model was based on the idea that every offender was ill and in need of treatment.

127) What is the term used to describe the phenomenon of recurring crime?

A) Reoffensive
B) Recidivism
C) The revolving door
D) None of the above

The correct answer is B:) Recidivism. Recidivism is used to study the frequency that offenders re-offend.

128) Who is recognized as the first American probation officer?

A) William Penn
B) Jacob Allison
C) Sir Robert Peel
D) None of the above

The correct answer is D:) None of the above. The first U.S. probation officer was John Augustus.

129) Special conditions of probation can include:

A) Those things that a judge thinks are necessary for a specific offender
B) Random drug screens
C) Treatment
D) All of the above

The correct answer is D:) All of the above. A judge imposes special conditions like these that are tailored to fit the offender and her needs.

130) Which of the following Constitutional Amendments was invoked in the case of Gideon v. Wainwright?

A) Fourth
B) Eighth
C) Tenth
D) Fourteenth

The correct answer is D:) Fourteenth. The Supreme Court ruled that under the due process clause of the Fourteenth Amendment if a defendant was too poor to hire an attorney the court must appoint one in any criminal case.

131) What was significant about Griffin v. Wisconsin (1987)?

A) It ruled that probation officers can search their offenders homes without search warrants.
B) It found that both notice and a hearing were required when pursuing revocation.
C) Established that probationers facing revocation were entitled to an attorney.
D) Decided that it was not necessary for a paroling authority to divulge reasons for not granting parole.

The correct answer is A:) It ruled that probation officers can search their offenders homes without search warrants. Officers do not need warrants or probable cause when searching the home of their probationers.

132) What was significant about Greenholtz v. Nebraska (1979)?

A) It ruled that probation officers can search their offenders homes without search warrants.
B) It found that both notice and a hearing were required when pursuing revocation.
C) Established that probationers facing revocation were entitled to an attorney.
D) Decided that it was not necessary for a paroling authority to divulge reasons for not granting parole.

The correct answer is D:) Decided that it was not necessary for a paroling authority to divulge reasons for not granting parole. Although knowing why could be helpful to the offender, it was not a requirement.

133) What was significant about Gagnon v. Scarpelli (1973)?

A) It ruled that probation officers can search their offenders homes without search warrants.
B) It found that both notice and a hearing were required when pursuing revocation.
C) Established that probationers facing revocation were entitled to an attorney.
D) Decided that it was not necessary for a paroling authority to divulge reasons for not granting parole.

The correct answer is C:) Established that probationers facing revocation were entitled to an attorney. This case also found that probationers were entitled to two hearings at revocation.

134) What was significant about Mempa v. Rhay (1967)?

A) It ruled that probation officers can search their offenders homes without search warrants.
B) It found that both notice and a hearing were required when pursuing revocation.
C) Established that probationers facing revocation were entitled to an attorney.
D) Decided that it was not necessary for a paroling authority to divulge reasons for not granting parole.

The correct answer is B:) It found that both notice and a hearing were required when pursuing revocation. This ruling overturned the previous case of Escoe v. Zerbst (1935).

135) What are intermediate sanctions?

A) Alternative sanctions
B) Sanctions that fall somewhere in between imprisonment and simple probation
C) Sanctions used in conjunction with a probationary term
D) All of the above

The correct answer is D:) All of the above. Intermediate sanctions are such things as house arrest, shock probation, and boot camps.

136) Which of the following requires the convicted offender to serve a period of incarceration followed by a period of probation?

    A) Shock probation
    B) Split sentence
    C) Suspended sentence
    D) None of the above

The correct answer is B:) Split sentence. This is an intermediate sanction.

137) Shock incarceration is typically used on which population?

    A) First time offenders
    B) Misdemeanor offenders
    C) Drug offenders
    D) None of the above

The correct answer is A:) First time offenders. This is used as an intermediate sanction designed to scare the offender away from future offenses.

138) What method is used to sentence only the most dangerous offenders?

    A) Retribution
    B) Selective incapacitation
    C) Selective deterrence
    D) General incapacitation

The correct answer is B:) Selective incapacitation. Selective incapacitation is one method used to combat overcrowding.

139) These facilities may resemble a college campus with low fences and heightened freedom of movement.

    A) Medium security
    B) Minimum security
    C) Maximum security
    D) Supermax

The correct answer is B:) Minimum security. These facilities allow offenders many of the freedoms they would miss in a more secure institution.

140) What is the term used to mean a temporary pass from a correctional institution into the community without supervision?

    A) A travel order
    B) Furlough
    C) Free pass
    D) Work release

The correct answer is B:) Furlough. Furloughs may be granted to offenders within minimum security institutions.

141) What process is used in prisons to account for all of the inmates?

    A) Counts
    B) Attendance
    C) Rosters
    D) None of the above

The correct answer is A:) Counts. Counts are used several times throughout the day to account for inmates.

142) Which of the following is true about prison disciplinary procedures?

    A) They are formal proceedings similar to a trial
    B) They are attended by an inmate's attorney
    C) They may result in visitation restrictions
    D) All of the above

The correct answer is C:) They may result in visitation restrictions. Inmates can lose several privileges as a result of a disciplinary rule violation.

143) Which of the following is a long term solitary confinement for dangerous inmates?

    A) Disciplinary segregation
    B) Administrative segregation
    C) Cell restriction
    D) None of the above

The correct answer is B:) Administrative segregation. This solitary confinement is marked by occasional reviews.

144) The archaic procedure of punishing an offender by extreme means and expecting God to intervene if the offender is innocent was referred to as:

A) Extreme incapacitation
B) Divine allowance
C) Trial by ordeal
D) None of the above

The correct answer is C:) Trial by ordeal. Trial by ordeal often involved extreme measures of torture.

145) Which state was the last one to abolish the electric chair as their sole means of execution?

A) North Dakota
B) Texas
C) Nebraska
D) Kansas

The correct answer is C:) Nebraska. Nebraska abolished execution by electric chair in February 2008.

146) Which of the following BEST describes restitution?

A) Imprisonment is the just punishment for committing a crime.
B) Criminals should be forced to compensate victims for any damage they inflicted.
C) Imprisonment allows an opportunity for criminals to be reeducated and introduced into society.
D) None of the above

The correct answer is B:) Criminals should be forced to compensate victims for any damage they inflicted. The theory of restitution takes the viewpoint that the commission of a crime was in infringing another individual's rights.

147) Which state leads the nation in the amount of executions it holds annually?

A) North Dakota
B) Texas
C) Nebraska
D) Kansas

The correct answer is B:) Texas. In 2006 Texas executed 26 of the 42 national executions.

148) Why are drugs a problem for prison administration?

    A) Increased medical costs
    B) Corruption of staff
    C) Heightened tensions among inmates
    D) All of the above

The correct answer is D:) All of the above. Drugs cause many problems for prison officials.

149) Which of the following best describes the case of Marbury v. Madison?

    A) Police entered and searched the defendant's home without a warrant. As a result, the evidence was deemed inadmissible in court under the Fourth Amendment.
    B) The defendant argued that he had a right to an appointment made by a previous President, and the Supreme Court agreed and established the power of judicial review.
    C) The defendant could not afford a lawyer and the Supreme Court ruled that under the Fourteenth Amendment the court must appoint a lawyer in all criminal cases in which this is the case.
    D) Eight boys were sentenced to death after being rushed through a trial and receiving no chance to consult defense. The Supreme Court ruled that States must ensure due process.

The correct answer is B:) The defendant argued that he had a right to an appointment made by a previous President, and the Supreme Court agreed and established the power of judicial review.

150) Prison gangs are typically divided among _____ lines.

    A) Racial
    B) Economic
    C) Geographical
    D) None of the above

The correct answer is A:) Racial. Prison gangs are similar to street gangs in that they are often divided among racial lines.

151) When must a suspect be read their Miranda Rights?

    A) Before they are taken into custody or questioned in any way.
    B) After they are taken into custody and before they are questioned.
    C) Before they are sentenced in court.
    D) At any point before their trial.

The correct answer is B:) After they are taken into custody and before they are questioned. This way they can be protected against self-incrimination during questioning.

152) The increase in elderly inmates is known as the:

    A) Gray wave
    B) Graying of the prisons
    C) The thin gray line
    D) None of the above

The correct answer is B:) Graying of the prisons. Elderly inmates pose many problems to prisons.

153) In the case Washington State v. Harper, the Supreme Court ruled:

    A) Elderly inmates could be euthanized upon request
    B) Mentally ill patients could not be forced to take medications
    C) Mentally ill patients could be forced to take medications
    D) Mentally ill patients were to be kept separate from the general population whenever possible

The correct answer is C:) Mentally ill patients could be forced to take medications. The Supreme Court voted to assist prison officials in the management of mentally ill inmates.

154) This early juvenile detention method attempted to put youth in an environment similar to a Christian family home:

    A) Reform houses
    B) Chicago Reform School
    C) Youth detention centers
    D) Houses of refuge

The correct answer is B:) Chicago Reform School. This school attempted to recreate a family environment for juvenile offenders.

155) Which term refers to those who have committed an offense that is only a crime due to the offender's age?

A) Juvenile offenses
B) Status offenses
C) Laws of reason
D) None of the above

The correct answer is B:) Status offenses. These are offenses like truancy.

156) What is the national organization responsible for juvenile crime data?

A) Office of Juvenile Justice and Delinquency Prevention
B) National Agency of Juvenile Statistics
C) Department of Juvenile Affairs
D) Organization for Delinquency Prevention

The correct answer is A:) Office of Juvenile Justice and Delinquency Prevention. This organization is referred to by the acronym OJJDP.

157) What was concluded by the Kansas City Patrol experiment?

A) Visible police presence has little impact on crime levels and resources should be shifted to more effective activities.
B) Visible police presence has a high impact on crime levels and more resources should be given to patrol units.
C) Visible police presence has the effect of actually increasing crime levels, and the practice should be avoided.
D) Visible police presence makes citizens feel less safe and the practice should be avoided.

The correct answer is A:) Visible police presence has little impact on crime levels and resources should be shifted to more effective activities. Not only did visible police presence not reduce crime, but citizens did not notice the change, or feel safer when they were present regularly.

158) What is the term used to refer to juveniles who have broken the law?

    A) Delinquent
    B) Dependant
    C) Undisciplined
    D) Neglected

The correct answer is A:) Delinquent. Juvenile delinquents are those who have actually broken a law.

159) Which policing style places an emphasis on arrests and citations, with the letter of the law being the most important factor?

    A) Authoritarian
    B) Legalistic
    C) Watchman
    D) Service

The correct answer is B:) Legalistic. The legalistic style also considers there to be one standard for all individuals, rather than recognizing differences in individual situations.

160) Which state created the first juvenile court?

    A) California
    B) Utah
    C) New York
    D) Illinois

The correct answer is D:) Illinois.

161) Which term translates to "father of the people"?

    A) Parens patriae
    B) Stare decisis
    C) Actus reas
    D) Voir dire

The correct answer is A:) Parens patriae. *Parens patriae* translates to "father of the people" and refers not only to the head of the household, but the role of government. This principle allowed for the King (or his representatives) to step in as a paternal figure in the lives of juveniles who broke the law. This meant that the King was the father over the country and subsequently had parental rights over all of the citizens.

162) Which of the following is NOT a Part I crime?

  A) Murder
  B) Burglary
  C) Embezzlement
  D) Rape

The correct answer is C:) Embezzlement. The original seven index crimes were: murder, rape, robbery, aggravated assault, larceny-theft, burglary, and motor vehicle theft. In 1979 an eighth crime was added to the index: arson.

163) Which of the following determined that unless a uniform policy of determining who is eligible for capital punishment exists, the death penalty will be regarded as cruel and unusual punishment?

  A) Hudson v. Palmer
  B) Gregg v. Georgia
  C) Furman v. Georgia
  D) Atkins v. Virginia

The correct answer is C:) Furman v. Georgia.

164) The FBI database containing DNA information is called what

  A) CNB
  B) INTERPOL
  C) PRUFOS
  D) CODIS

The correct answer is D:) CODIS. The FBI uses and administers a large DNA database referred to as CODIS which stands for Combined DNA Index System.

165) At what point is bail set?

  A) Arrest
  B) Trial
  C) Arraignment
  D) Sentencing

The correct answer is C:) Arraignment. Bail is set by the judge at the arraignment.

166) Administrative law covers which of the following?

   A) EPA
   B) OSHA
   C) FBI
   D) All of the above

The correct answer is D:) All of the above.

167) Which of the following is under the supervision of the DHS?

   A) EPA
   B) OSHA
   C) FAMS
   D) UCR

The correct answer is C:) FAMS. The Federal Air Marshal Service (FAMS) is an agency which operates under the Department of Homeland Security. Its purpose is to ensure the safety of individuals in the United States traveling by plane by identifying and deterring hostile or terrorist acts which occur on planes.

168) When a teen first exhibits delinquent behavior it is referred to as

   A) Age of onset
   B) Disparity
   C) Clearance rate
   D) None of the above

The correct answer is A:) Age of onset. Age of onset is the age at which a child/teen first exhibits delinquent behavior of a criminal nature. The earlier the age of onset, the more frequent, varied and long lasting the criminal career.

Test-Taking Strategies

Here are some test-taking strategies that are specific to this test and to other DSST tests in general:

- Keep your eyes on the time. Pay attention to how much time you have left.

- Read the entire question and read all the answers. Many questions are not as hard to answer as they may seem. Sometimes, a difficult sounding question really only is asking you how to read an accompanying chart. Chart and graph questions are on most DANTES/DSST tests and should be an easy free point.

- If you don't know the answer immediately, the new computer-based testing lets you mark questions and come back to them later if you have time.

- Read the wording carefully. Some words can give you hints to the right answer. There are no exceptions to an answer when there are words in the question such as always, all or none. If one of the answer choices includes most or some of the right answers, but not all, then that is not the answer. Here is an example:

  The primary colors include all of the following:

  A) Red, Yellow, Blue, Green

  B) Red, Green, Yellow

  C) Red, Orange, Yellow

  D) Red, Yellow, Blue

  Although item A includes all the right answers, it also includes an incorrect answer, making it incorrect. If you didn't read it carefully, was in a hurry, or didn't know the material well, you might fall for this.

- Make a guess on a question that you do not know the answer to. There is no penalty for an incorrect answer. Eliminate the answer choices that you know are incorrect. For example, this will let your guess be a 1 in 3 chance instead.

Test Preparation

How much you need to study depends on your knowledge of a subject area. If you are interested in literature, took it in school, or enjoy reading then your study and preparation for the literature or humanities test will not need to be as intensive as that of someone who is new to literature.

This book is much different than the regular DANTES study guides. This book actually teaches you the information that you need to know to pass the test. If you are particularly interested in an area, or feel that you want more information, do a quick search online. We've tried not to include too much depth in areas that are not as essential on the test. Everything in this book will be on the test. It is important to understand all major theories and concepts listed in the table of contents. It is also important to know any bolded words.

Don't worry if you do not understand or know a lot about the area. With minimal study, you can complete and pass the test.

 # Legal Note

FLASHCARDS

This section contains flashcards for you to use to further your understanding of the material and test yourself on important concepts, names or dates. Read the term or question then flip the page over to check the answer on the back. Keep in mind that this information may not be covered in the text of the study guide. Take your time to study the flashcards, you will need to know and understand these concepts to pass the test.

Mens rea

Actus reas

Penal code

Case law works under
the law of what?

Criminology

Positivist theory was
developed by

Biological theory of crime

Social learning theory

Guilty act

Guilty mind

Precedent

Written and organized laws

Cesare Lombroso

The scientific study of crime and applicable criminal theories

When we learn what is acceptable from the people around us

The belief that a criminal gene is present in people who commit crime

Control theory examines what?

Misdemeanor

Felony

Treason

White collar crime

Victimless crime

When a family member commits a crime against another family member

UCR

A relatively minor offense, punishable by a fine or up to one year incarceration

What keeps people from committing a crime

A United States citizen who conspires with another country to in some way harm, wage war, or overthrow the United States Government

Offense that is punishable by death or more than one year incarceration

Crimes where there seems to be no victim, such as prostitution or gambling

Fraud, including crimes include embezzlement, credit card and check fraud, insurance fraud, bribes, tax evasion, kickbacks, and computer-related crime

Uniform Crime Report

Domestic crime

Dark figure of crime

NCVS

NIBRS

Patria postestas

Opportunity theory

Kent v. U.S.

In Re Gault

Code of Hammurabi

National Crime
Victimization Survey

Crimes that are never
reported to police

The father of the
household had absolute
control over everyone else
in the household

National Incident-Based
Reporting System

Landmark case making the
rules for moving or keeping
a juvenile's court case
in juvenile court or trying
them as an adult

Juvenile delinquency
is due to the lack of
opportunities provided to
lower class youth

Earliest known laws

Laid the groundwork for
right to counsel, protection
from self-incrimination,
right to confront witnesses,
and notice of charges

Common law	Mala prohibita
Who was the Warren Court known for?	Brown v. Board of Education
Gideon v. Wainwright	Mapp v. Ohio
Miranda v. Arizona	Abbington v. Schemmp

Laws that are on the books but may not be considered immoral if it weren't for the statute calling it so

An unwritten body of law

Segregation, civil rights

The Supreme court led by Chief Justice Earl Warren who was very concerned with protecting the people against the power of the government in criminal proceedings

Search and seizure

Right to counsel

Separation of church and state

Rights of the accused

Katz v. United States

Substantive due process

Procedural due process

Due process model

A group of ten tithings

Hue and Cry method

Frankpledge system

DEA

The creation and definition of what a person's rights are

Search and seizure, wiretaps

Protecting individual rights at all stages in the Criminal Justice process

The enforcement of the laws and the punishments for violations

Shout for others to hear something similar to "Thief, stop!"

A reeve

Drug enforcement agency

The guarantee of peace that each person gave the King

U.S. Marshals are in charge of what?

Occupational deviance

Abuse of authority

Jurisdiction

District court judges are appointed by who?

Circuit

Appeal

Barristers

Behavior that is motivated by personal gain

Conduct prisoner transports, arrest and pursue fugitives, provide security in Federal courts, and are personal security for Federal judges and magistrates

The locations, types, and subject matter of court cases over which a specific court has the power to preside

Acts that damage the goals of law enforcement

A group of federal judicial districts

The President of the United States

Another name for attorney

Request made to a higher court to review the findings of judgment from a lower court